MW00582759

EARLY ALABAMA

Alabama

THE FORGE OF HISTORY

A SERIES OF ILLUSTRATED GUIDES

Early ALABAMA

An
Illustrated Guide
to the
Formative Years,
1798–1826

◆ ◆ ◆

Mike Bunn

The University of Alabama Press / Tuscaloosa

The University of Alabama Press
Tuscaloosa, Alabama 35487-0380
uapress.ua.edu

Typeface: Adobe Garamond Pro / Myriad Pro

Manufactured in China
Cover images: *Top*, a depiction of the Vine and Olive Colony,
courtesy of the Alabama Department of Archives and History;
bottom, the Mississippi Territory in 1812, by Samuel Lewis
Cover design: Todd Lape / Lape Designs

Library of Congress Cataloging-in-Publication Data

Names: Bunn, Mike, author.
Title: Early Alabama : an illustrated guide to the formative years, 1798–1826 / Mike Bunn.
Description: Tuscaloosa : The University of Alabama Press, [2019] | Includes
bibliographical references and index.
Identifiers: LCCN 2018045775| ISBN 9780817359287 (pbk.) | ISBN 9780817392550 (ebook)
Subjects: LCSH: Alabama—History—To 1819. | Alabama—History—1819–1950.
Classification: LCC F326 .B93 2019 | DDC 976.1/01—dc23
LC record available at https://lccn.loc.gov/2018045775

For my grandmothers, Era Eugene Davis Bunn
and Mildred Juanita Ginn Knighton,
whose stories of growing up in the rural South
enthralled me as a child and helped spark an
endless fascination with the way things were

CONTENTS

ix ◆ List of Illustrations

xiii ◆ Acknowledgments

1 ◆ Introduction

5 ◆ *One* Before Alabama: The Mississippi Territory

19 ◆ *Two* Alabama in Flames: The Creek War and War of 1812

31 ◆ *Three* Alabama Fever: The Great Migration

47 ◆ *Four* Alabama: The Place and the People

59 ◆ *Five* The Land Called Alabama: From Territory to State

73 ◆ *Six* Alabama: From Old Southwest to Old South

87 ◆ Epilogue

91 ◆ Historic Sites Tour

133 ◆ Notes

149 ◆ Bibliography

163 ◆ Index

ILLUSTRATIONS

7 ◆ The Mississippi Territory in 1812
9 ◆ Map of Mississippi and the Alabama Territory, 1818
12 ◆ Governor Winthrop Sargent
13 ◆ Assembly Hall in Washington, Mississippi
15 ◆ Aaron Burr
16 ◆ Tecumseh
20 ◆ Sketch of Fort Mims
22 ◆ The attack on Fort Mims
23 ◆ The Canoe Fight
24 ◆ The Battle of Autossee
25 ◆ General Andrew Jackson
27 ◆ The Battle of Horseshoe Bend
29 ◆ The attack on Fort Bowyer in September 1814
32 ◆ The Tennessee River at Florence
33 ◆ Drawing of a stagecoach
36 ◆ Henry Hitchcock
40 ◆ Depiction of the Vine and Olive Colony
42 ◆ A slave coffle on the road
44 ◆ Runaway slave advertisement from the *Blakeley Sun*
49 ◆ The John Looney House
54 ◆ Depiction of a frontier camp meeting
55 ◆ Site of the "Big Spring" in downtown Huntsville
57 ◆ Modern downtown Mobile
57 ◆ Map of a portion of Blakeley
60 ◆ Map showing the territory ceded by the Creeks
62 ◆ Map of Alabama Territory, 1818
63 ◆ Governor William Wyatt Bibb

66 ◆ Land ceded in Alabama by Indian tribes, 1806–35
69 ◆ Upper Creek Chief Opothle Yoholo
71 ◆ Reconstruction of the cabinet shop in Huntsville where the constitutional convention met in 1819
74 ◆ President James Monroe
78 ◆ Depiction of the capitol at Cahawba
79 ◆ Governor Israel Pickens
81 ◆ Image from a notice by the Steamboat Company of Alabama
83 ◆ The Marquis de Lafayette
86 ◆ The state capitol building in Tuscaloosa, ca. 1840
91 ◆ Alabama and Mississippi
92 ◆ Natchez
92 ◆ Mississippi River at Natchez
94 ◆ House on Ellicott Hill
94 ◆ Auburn
96 ◆ Site of Forks of the Road Slave Market
97 ◆ Historic Jefferson College
99 ◆ North Alabama
99 ◆ The Stagecoach Inn and Tavern
100 ◆ Weeden House
102 ◆ Joel Eddins House
103 ◆ Pope's Tavern and Museum
104 ◆ First Presbyterian Church
105 ◆ Overton Farm cabin
106 ◆ North central Alabama
107 ◆ The King House
108 ◆ Murphree log cabin
110 ◆ Central Alabama
111 ◆ Lucas Tavern
112 ◆ Museum of Alabama
113 ◆ Grave of William Wyatt Bibb
115 ◆ Fort Toulouse – Fort Jackson Park
116 ◆ West central Alabama
117 ◆ Log cabin at Bluff Hall
119 ◆ Saint James CME Church
121 ◆ The Old Tavern
122 ◆ Umbria Schoolhouse
123 ◆ East Alabama

123 ◆ Horseshoe Bend National Military Park
125 ◆ South Alabama
126 ◆ Condé-Charlotte House
127 ◆ The Ellicott Stone
128 ◆ Historic Blakeley State Park
129 ◆ Fort Mims State Historic Site
131 ◆ Old Saint Stephens Historical Park
132 ◆ Masonic Lodge #3

ACKNOWLEDGMENTS

As anyone who has ever written a book well knows, there are always more people the author should thank than space and time allow. Below I have attempted to list the names of those people and institutions that have been especially pivotal in making this project become a reality. Some rendered very practical assistance, while others served as inspiration.

First, I would like to thank Linda Manning, Dan Waterman, Donna Cox Baker, and the entire staff of the University of Alabama Press for entrusting me with the responsibility of telling this important chapter of state history as we celebrate the bicentennial of Alabama's statehood. A special thanks is also in order for copyeditor Dawn Hall, whose attention to detail improved the manuscript and is greatly appreciated. I would like to thank Scotty Kirkland of the Alabama Department of Archives and History (ADAH), who helped facilitate my writing about the era for *Alabama Heritage* magazine, a circumstance that ultimately led to the writing of this book. Scotty generously made available reams of information that I used in my research and graciously assisted with several inquiries. Indeed, lest I forget someone, I would like to thank the entirety of the staff at ADAH for their assistance during various phases of research.

Several other individuals were instrumental in the course of this project. I appreciate Rachel Dobson for taking a few photographs of sites in and around Tuscaloosa for me; Raven Christopher for providing information on a fascinating structure in downtown Mobile; and Nan Prince for help in securing images from the collections of the Mississippi Department of Archives and History. I appreciate my friends Steve and Julie Hooper for allowing me to use their home as a base of operations during some of my travels for research in north Alabama as well as taking me to a few historic spots of interest. Dr. Robert Mellown, now retired from a distinguished teaching career at the University of Alabama, kindly reviewed portions of the book concerning the architectural heritage of the period under study and made available some images that improved it. Bob Peck at the Historic Mobile Preservation Society's Minnie Mitchell Archives is one of the most knowledgeable and courteous volunteers with whom I have had the pleasure to work. The staffs of the Marx Library at the University of South Alabama, the Daphne Public Library, the Mobile Public Library, the Huntsville Public Library, and the Ralph Brown Draughon Library at Auburn University were consistently helpful as well. I also appreciate the staff of the University of Alabama's Cartographic Research Laboratory, which graciously provided several custom maps featured in the book.

I sincerely appreciate the advice and suggestions offered by the people who read the first drafts of this narrative: my colleague and friend Clay Williams, who helped draft the summary of the Creek War we first published in our book *Battle for the Southern Frontier: The Creek War and the War of 1812*, which forms the basis for much of chapter 2 of this publication; acclaimed Mobile historian, gifted writer, and genuine gentleman John Sledge; and former ADAH director Ed Bridges, a true paragon of information on all things relating to Alabama history. I particularly appreciate the suggestions and encouragement of Dr. Gregory Waselkov, a ridiculously busy and talented man who took the time to help me improve the final draft and offered assistance at several points.

I would also like to offer a special thanks to two of the incredible historians I had the good fortune to study under during my college years and whose influence on my career is enduring: Dr. Ed Hicks of Faulkner University, who encouraged me to pursue my passion as a vocation; and the late Dr. Forrest McDonald, who in one of the last courses he taught at the University of Alabama convinced me of the duty historians have to write and helped me understand how to do so more clearly. In a similar fashion, thanks are in order as well to the late Jo Ann Flirt, who convinced me to join the team at Historic Blakeley State Park and thus allowed me the luxury of working at one of Alabama's most treasured historic sites as I continue to research and write about the state's past. As always, I would like to thank my wife, Tonya, and daughter, Zoey, who indulge me the time to pursue the telling of historical tales such as this one.

Lastly, I feel I would be remiss if I did not acknowledge in some way the valuable work of the numerous scholars who have investigated early Alabama's history before me and whose work—some of it published over a century ago and some contemporary with my own—have in truth more than anyone made this book possible. Space precludes a complete listing of their names and merit, but anyone who is curious about the time period I explore here should know about the important work of individuals including Albert James Pickett, Willis Brewer, Thomas Perkins Abernethy, Peter J. Hamilton, Frank L. Owsley and Frank L. Owsley Jr., Jack D. L. Holmes, Harvey H. Jackson III, Gregory Waselkov, and Herbert James Lewis, just to name a few. It is an honor to be in your company.

INTRODUCTION

Alabama's rich history is studded with iconic moments familiar to even the most casual student of the past. From the triumphant entrance into Mobile Bay of Admiral David Farragut's fleet during the Civil War to the determined Selma to Montgomery march during the civil rights movement a century later, events of national importance have often played out on the state's storied landscape. Unfortunately, some of the events most fundamental in understanding the essence of Alabama, which took place during the state's territorial and early statehood years, are often unfamiliar to even those reasonably well acquainted with the state's history. In fact, the people, places, and events of the time period that shaped the young state into what it became are collectively hazily remembered as part of an era of random pioneer settlement, obscure wilderness taming, and reactionary Indian fighting. The major events of the period, to the extent they are known at all, are often understood devoid of rhyme, reason, or context. Many, if not most, people are still confused by the fact that what became Alabama was once part of a political unit called the Mississippi Territory, and are unaware that it became the primary theater of a brutal war that would forever change the course of regional history. They are often surprised to learn it was itself an independent United States territory for a brief time, uncertain of when and how Alabama entered the union, and astonished to discover the depth and breadth of settlement and political rancor in the future state prior to that event. More than any other epoch of Alabama's history, the basic facts of this part of the state's timeline escape us.

Further complicating matters is the fact that the era does not have a clear line of demarcation that separates it from what came after; the antebellum era ends neatly with the onset of the Civil War, for example, the Great Depression era with World War II, and so on. Nor do the territorial and early statehood years seem to fit naturally with the ensuing antebellum time period even though the two are often lumped together in the state's historical timeline. The early statehood era featured more small farms and log cabins than large plantations, for starters, not to mention the era included the presence of large Native American communities soon to be removed from their ancient homeland and thus Alabama's historical drama. It is even hard for us to imagine in our mind's eye life in early Alabama in some ways, since, as compared to the relatively abundant surviving architecture of the later antebellum period, extraordinarily little of early Alabama's built environment survives. In short, Alabama's founding era seems remote to most of the general public—few familiar stories, fewer recognizable characters, even fewer extant landmarks.

Alabama's territorial and early statehood period forms a distinct era in its history, however, and deserves to be appreciated and understood on its own terms. The pattern of development that time period witnessed set in motion all that would come after, influencing for generations such basic aspects of Alabama's development as the functioning of its economy, patterns of land use, the location of communities, and the form and substance of political rivalries. It simultaneously set the tone and tenor for the society that grew within its borders. There is much to be admired in this story of coming of age, but there is also much to be regretted. The pioneering spirit that animated the state's early American settlers to lay Alabama's foundation, after all, at the same time facilitated the rise of a society built in no small part at the expense of the area's native inhabitants and the forced labor of enslaved African Americans.

This book is intended to be an introduction to the people, places, and events of Alabama's territorial and early statehood years. It is not an academic treatise or a comparative study of Alabama's place in the world in which it was birthed. Rather, in a fast-paced, overview-fashion narrative divided into six short chapters, the book chronicles, through a distinctly local lens, Alabama's formative years. It chronicles the state's origins as the remote and neglected "backwoods" of the Mississippi Territory, the watershed conflict known as the Creek War that raged across it in 1813–14, the fabled "Great Migration" to Alabama in the war's aftermath, the people and culture of early Alabama, the state's brief period as an independent territory and heady pursuit of statehood, and its entrance into the union and the landmark events of its first years as a state. For purposes of this study I have defined the territorial and early statehood period as spanning from 1798, the year of the Mississippi Territory's formation, to 1826, the year that the state capital moved from the town of Cahawba (later known as Cahaba) to Tuscaloosa. At the end of the narrative is a tour of historic sites associated with the era throughout the state and beyond that comprises the great majority of the publicly accessible structures dating to the time period and relevant to this story that are still standing. A few privately owned structures are included as well. Selected battlefields, historic markers, museums, and other historic sites that those interested in exploring this era in state history may wish to visit are also included.

It is my hope that the narrative and tour will work together to encourage a greater appreciation of Alabama's territorial and early statehood years and facilitate discovery of a largely forgotten but fascinating and crucial saga in the state's past. While most of the structures Alabama's founders and early inhabitants built are long gone, the landscape that drew them here, and from which they drew sustenance, remains. By exploring it with an eye toward the past we gain a unique understanding of the time and place we can acquire in perhaps no other way. To understand Alabama's territorial and early statehood years, after all, is to understand its very roots.

One

BEFORE ALABAMA

The Mississippi Territory

After a long period as a province claimed by various colonial powers, Alabama's road toward statehood began in 1798 with the formation of the Mississippi Territory. The future state would eventually be carved from the eastern half of the territory. Slow growth, a disunited government, sectional rivalry, and international intrigue plagued the region in its first decade of existence.

The land that became Alabama once lay at the heart of the original American Southwest. Literally south and west of the more established Atlantic seaboard states, the region existed throughout the revolutionary period until well into the nineteenth century as a frontier borderland on the periphery of the mainstream of American cultural, political, and economic life. Relatively remote and containing a small American population, most of the area lay in Native American hands until well into the territorial years despite the grand claims of ownership by various European powers and the nascent American government.

Although Spanish explorers had surveyed its coastline or trekked through what became Alabama as early as the first half of the sixteenth century, it had been the French who conducted the first sustained efforts at colonization beginning in 1702 with the founding of Mobile. That initial experiment in settlement launched a century of European involvement in what became Alabama. From their Gulf Coast administrative centers, the French claimed to oversee an enormous swath of the North American continent, but in truth they had little presence in Alabama beyond its coastal areas during their six decades as the preeminent colonial power in the region. In 1763 the British acquired all lands the French claimed in North America as a result of France's defeat in the French and Indian War. The British incorporated the southern half of the future state of Alabama into the colony of West Florida during their administration of the region, but they, like the French before them, likewise had little presence in the land north of Mobile outside of a few scattered and lightly manned military outposts.[1]

During the Revolutionary War, Spain seized the opportunity to take the lightly defended area from the distracted British and claimed by conquest all of Florida after seizing forts at Pensacola, Mobile, and along the Mississippi River. Spain thus replaced the British as the colonial authority in nominal control of what would become Alabama beginning in 1783. Spain had little more presence in the region than its predecessors, though, and by 1795 had yielded to American pressure to pull back from its claims to territory above the 31st parallel—just north of Mobile—in the Treaty of San Lorenzo. Local authorities headquartered at Natchez along the Mississippi River refused to comply with the treaty at first, however, using a variety of delaying tactics in the hope the compact might be overturned. At length acquiescing, American forces finally took control of all Spanish territory north of the 31st parallel in March 1798.[2]

On April 7, 1798, President John Adams approved the act of Congress creating the Mississippi Territory from this land. Congress officially placed its northern boundary at the point where the Yazoo River emptied into the Mississippi, or 32°28′ latitude. At this time surveyor Andrew Ellicott had already begun his work marking the southern boundary, between the United States and Spanish Florida, which stretched along the 31st parallel from the Mississippi in the west to the Chattahoochee in the east. In 1804 Congress would add to this rectangular strip of land all the territory south of Tennessee and lying between the Mississippi and Georgia's western boundary once Georgia relinquished its long-standing claims to the region. Citing its colonial charter of 1732, Georgia had long claimed dubious title to land stretching all the way to the Mississippi. At least three times in the late 1700s, various officials attempted to sanction the disposal of some of these western lands for profit, with a particularly corrupt scheme known as the Yazoo Fraud hatched in 1795,

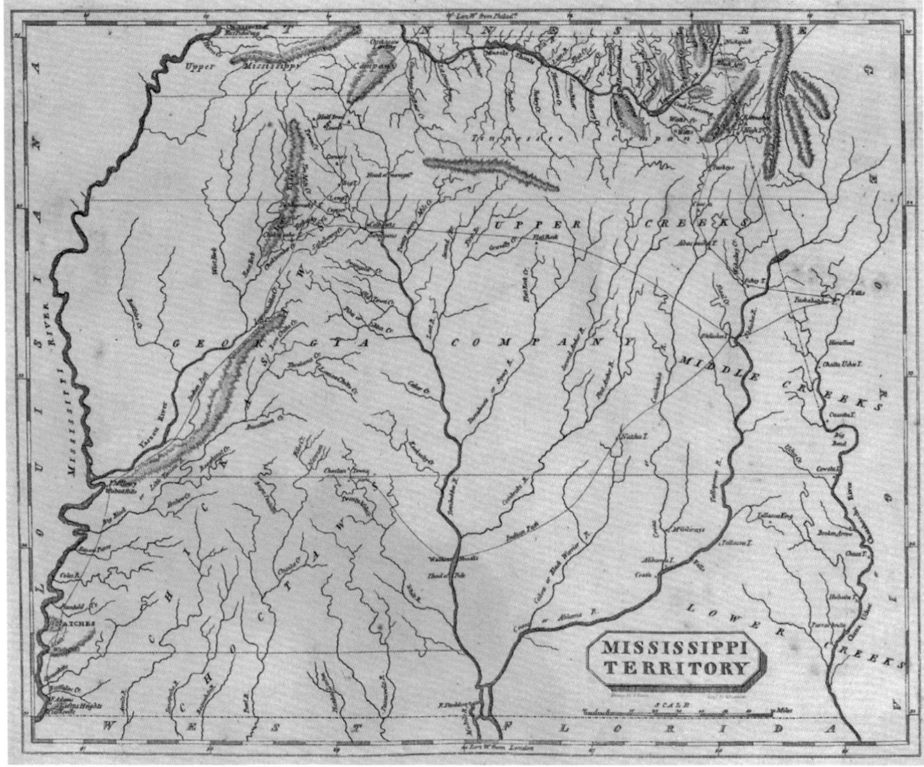

The Mississippi Territory in 1812, by Samuel Lewis, showing the territory below the 31st parallel still in the possession of the Spanish. Courtesy of the David Rumsey Map Collection.

which featured outright bribery of public officials to push the deal through. While the Georgia legislature rescinded the act a year later, the issue took years for Congress to sort out.[3]

The Mississippi Territory's borders remained in this situation until the War of 1812, when the United States annexed portions of what had been Spanish West Florida. Residents of the territory had never been comfortable with foreign lands lying along their southern border and separating them from the gulf, into which most the region's major rivers emptied. Not only did colonial authorities hamper economic life in the territory by arbitrarily closing ports or imposing onerous export duties on shipping, residents also feared they worked to incite Indians to resistance of American settlement of the region. In a rather flimsy but convenient attempt to annex West Florida prior to the War of 1812, American officials and local residents claimed as early as 1804 that the Spanish colony belonged to the United States via the terms of the Louisiana Purchase signed in 1803. Rebellions and rumors of uprisings flared along the border for nearly a decade afterward. Following a successful insurgency in the westernmost portion of the colony in 1810—what has become known in history as the West Florida Rebellion—American officials on paper proclaimed the annexation of the entirety of Spanish territory stretching between the Mississippi and the Perdido Rivers. The Spanish tacitly acknowledged the loss of land west of the Pearl River by making no effort to reclaim it but refused to remove troops from the administrative center of Mobile. Less than a year after the United States declared war on Spain's ally, Great Britain, in 1812, General James Wilkinson arrived at Mobile with a combined army and navy force and demanded the surrender of Fort Carlota, ostensibly to prevent the outpost from supplying aid to Britain. Outmanned and outgunned, the small Spanish garrison surrendered without firing a shot. The portion of West Florida lying between the Pearl and the Perdido was at last under American control and was immediately incorporated into the Mississippi Territory.[4]

This enormous swath of the southwestern frontier, stretching fully from the Tennessee state line to the Gulf of Mexico and from the Chattahoochee to the Mississippi Rivers, included some of the choicest agricultural land on the continent. Little of it had been cleared for that purpose when it first came under American control, though, outside of scattered small Native American plots. Dense forests with ancient hardwoods and pines dominated most of the landscape, their "depths the last rays of the sun could scarcely penetrate," according to one traveler, and they offered the promise of ample building material at a time when wooden construction predominated. Thick vegetation of all sorts covered the land's surface; canebrakes so dense a man could not enter them, and flowers, shrubs, and vines innumerable proliferated throughout the region. Tall grasses grew in the meadows that opened between patches of forest. A wide variety of indigenous fruits, edible greens, and vegetables grew across the new territory. With its mild climate, abundant rainfall, and series of rivers capable of supporting trade between the fertile interior and the coastal outlets, the Mississippi Territory appeared rich with potential.[5]

Almost all of the region's great promise as part of the expanding American union lay as unrealized potential until well into the territorial period, however. The "Americanization" of the future state of Alabama proceeded slowly, in truth not beginning in earnest until after the War of 1812. Alabama in 1811 therefore in some respects had more in common with its appearance in 1711 than the burgeoning new state that would enter the American union less than a decade later. As late as 1810, only a few isolated, widely separated pockets

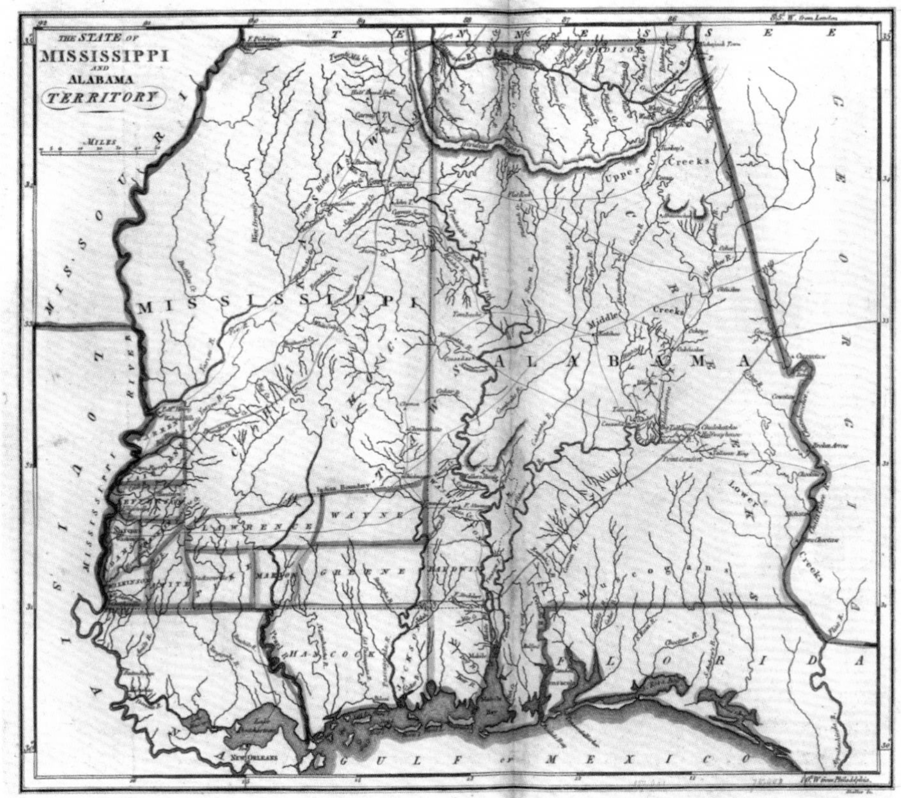

Map of Mississippi and the Alabama Territory, 1818, by Matthew Carey, showing the location of Natchez and the Tombigbee settlements, and the portion of Spanish West Florida added to the territory after the War of 1812. Courtesy of the David Rumsey Map Collection.

of non-Indian settlement existed on small tracts within the territory. These had been occupied with the official permission of Native Americans. In the western portion of the Mississippi Territory, along its namesake Mississippi River, a particularly desirable triangular tract known as the Natchez District had emerged as the primary of the two regions of the territory with any sizable American population. The district's European settlement dated to the colonial era, but during the Revolutionary War era, hundreds of loyalists and various other land seekers found their way there at the invitation of the Spanish, who hoped to build up the area's population as a buffer to encroachment on their other colonial landholdings. Its legal settlement by Americans was confirmed by the 1801 Treaty of Fort Adams with the Choctaws. Along with the city of Natchez, developing settlements at Walnut Hills (Vicksburg), Port Gibson, and

Woodville sprang up in and adjacent to the district as some of the Mississippi Territory's earliest American cities worthy of the title. Natchez, originally laid out by the Spanish in the 1780s along a high bluff on the Mississippi but tracing its history back to a military outpost of French in the early 1700s, emerged as by far the largest commercial and population center in the area. In the first decade of the nineteenth century it ranked as the largest city between New Orleans and the Ohio Valley and had already established itself as the territory's one true metropolis. Natchez in truth could be described as two closely associated communities, one a sophisticated urban center on the bluff and the other a gritty river port known as Natchez-Under-the-Hill. Altogether Natchez featured a concentration of business activity, cultural endeavors, and political power unrivaled anywhere in the Southwest throughout most of the territorial period.[6]

In the eastern section of the territory lay the lone other area of concentrated American settlement in the form of a series of farmsteads, plantations, and coalescing small communities along the Tensaw River and the lower reaches of the Alabama and Tombigbee north of Mobile. Similar to the Natchez District in that its non-Indian settlement dated to the colonial era with the permission of the Choctaw and the Creeks, it also had become the destination of loyalists and various other traders and opportunists with the blessing of the Spanish after the revolutionary era. Even though these settlements featured no true cities, they would compose virtually the entirety of American influence in what would become Alabama for nearly the first decade of the Mississippi Territory's existence. In fact, the first county in the future state, Washington, would have as its nucleus some of this area of settlement even though its original boundaries technically encompassed a wide expanse of land stretching all the way from the Pearl River in what is today Mississippi to the Chattahoochee. Around 1806, following the negotiation of treaties with the Cherokee and Chickasaw in the northern extremity of the territory, a section of the "Big Bend" of the Tennessee River would be opened for settlement and lead to the creation of a second area of American presence in the future state. Its settlement would be so rapid that within five years the area, including Madison County and its principal city, Huntsville, would be on the path to preeminence in the eastern section of the Mississippi Territory. In the remainder of the hinterland of the future state prior to 1810, though, the only other significant American presence lay in the form of the homesteads of a few Indian countrymen, independent traders who had chosen to establish themselves among the area's native communities and who often married Indian women. Perhaps the best-documented of this small group of a few dozen individuals living in what became Alabama at the time is Abraham Mordecai, a Jewish trader who had settled near the future site of Montgomery as early as 1785 and who is credited with the introduction of the first cotton gin into Alabama.[7]

On its creation of the Mississippi Territory, Congress established a makeshift government at Natchez copied from that of the Northwest Territory (established in 1787). This government featured a limited number of appointed officials. As soon as the territory reached a population of five thousand free male inhabitants, it could transition to a second stage of territorial government featuring a bicameral legislature with members of the lower house popularly elected. It would also at that time be granted a congressional delegate. President John Adams appointed stern New Englander Winthrop Sargent as the territory's first governor. Perceived as haughty and out of touch with the needs of the region's settlers, Sargent proved unpopular from the start. The other officials appointed by federal authorities to assist him in establishing a government were late to arrive, which only made matters worse, as their tardiness literally forced Sargent to govern by himself at times. Discontent with the governor only grew in the wake of his attempt to codify the laws of the territory in 1799. Local detractors disparaged the laws as unconstitutional and derisively referred to them as "Sargent's Code." Bowing to mounting local complaints, in 1800 Congress authorized the territory to proceed to the second stage of government despite not having reached the population requirement that would legally allow it to do so. Later that year when Thomas Jefferson won election as president, he replaced Sargent with the ambitious twenty-six-year-old rising political star W. C. C. Claiborne.[8]

Claiborne's administration would move the Mississippi Territory forward on a number of fronts but be plagued by variations of the pervasive factionalism and infighting that had doomed Sargent. The governor helped further organize the territory by the creation of new counties and organization of a militia and by initiating concerted efforts to resolve the tangle of conflicting land claims in portions of the region that cruelly vexed both territorial and federal officials. In some areas, French, Spanish, English, and American grants overlapped on the same piece of property and thus impeded settlement. Claiborne found developing consensus within his politically divided government to be difficult, despite his tact and diplomacy, as party politics and an ongoing Republican-Federalist feud shadowed the governor's every decision. The partisan rancor is best exemplified by the movement of the territorial capital. In one of the first acts of the new territorial legislature after Claiborne's appointment, the newly empowered local Republican Party affiliates had

Governor Winthrop Sargent. Courtesy of the Mississippi Department of Archives and History.

chosen to move the territorial capital from Natchez, perceived as a Federalist Party stronghold, to the tiny village of Washington—allegedly more suitable to Republican tastes—a mere six miles away. In 1803 President Thomas Jefferson sent Governor Claiborne to New Orleans to accept the transfer of the recently purchased Louisiana Territory (the Louisiana Purchase). He would not return; the next year he would be appointed as first governor of the newly created Orleans Territory.[9]

Assembly Hall in Washington, meeting place of the Mississippi Territory's legislature, as it appeared before being destroyed in a fire in the 1990s. Courtesy of the Library of Congress.

Native North Carolinian Robert Williams served as the Mississippi Territory's next appointed executive, being elevated from his post as land commissioner to the executive office by President Jefferson. Preceded by acting interim governor Cato West and followed by another temporary de facto executive, Cowles Mead, Williams presided over one of the most tumultuous interludes in territorial affairs before abruptly resigning in apparent frustration at a thankless task in dealing with the organized factions working against him. Dissension reigned during Williams's tenure on a number of fronts, especially in the developing eastern section of the territory. Remote, overlooked, and having little contact with the seat of government along the Mississippi, the "backwoods"—practically the entirety of the territory east of the Pearl River—chafed at its neglect and in at least two respects threatened to take matters into its own hands counter to the wishes of authorities. First, in a development that would fester in regional political life for the better part of two decades, easterners began to advocate for the territory's division. As early as 1803 residents of the area that became Alabama sent formal petitions to Congress requesting they be allowed to establish a government separate from that in distant

Natchez. They claimed that the "settlements on the Mobile Tombecbee and Alabama rivers are composed of people different in their manners and customs, different in their interests, & nature appears never to have designed the two countries to be under the same Government." Second, filibusters and various other adventurers working with rebels along both sides of the border with West Florida began to scheme for ways to seize the colony from the Spanish, whom they deeply resented for their ability to control the gulf outlets of most of the region's navigable rivers. Efforts to monitor and prevent a full-blown international conflict along this largely unguarded and disaffected frontier thus occupied an increasing amount of time for territorial officials who had neither the means nor the manpower to exert their authority in the expansive region. In the hub of American settlement in the eastern section of the territory north of Mobile, for example, Judge Harry Toulmin served for many years as the lone representative of territorial government in many respects, fulfilling the roles of several offices simultaneously out of necessity.[10]

The general discontent and disorganization attracted intrigue. In perhaps the most famous political incident of the Mississippi Territory's first decade of existence, officials arrested none other than former Vice President Aaron Burr in what is now Alabama. Burr had fled Natchez, where he had been detained by a grand jury that in a turn of events that briefly became the talk of the nation, had considered whether or not to bring charges of treason against him. Burr, accompanied by a small flotilla of supporters, had arrived in the Natchez area in the winter of 1807 on a mission whose exact nature remains unclear to this day. It allegedly involved illegal annexation of territory at minimum or possibly even disunion and the creation of a new state. Officials in Washington County discovered Burr attempting to travel covertly through the region one night in February 1807, and General Edmund P. Gaines had him arrested at once. Authorities held Burr at Fort Stoddert for a short time before sending him under escort to Richmond, Virginia, where he later stood trial and won acquittal.[11]

Intrigue and factionalism among the Native Americans residing in the Mississippi Territory would come to have a more profound impact on the trajectory of the future state of Alabama than Burr's scheming. The territory's borders encompassed ancestral lands of the Cherokee, Chickasaw, Choctaw, and Creek, and in its first decade of existence native inhabitants outnumbered American settlers by a large margin. In the eastern section of the territory the Creeks held sway over approximately two-thirds of the region and exerted influence in even more despite alleged territorial government jurisdiction. They boasted a population of about twenty thousand people at a time when

Aaron Burr. Courtesy of the Library of Congress.

the total American residents of the area, free and slave, numbered less than half that. The Creek Nation was a loose confederacy of dozens of autonomous towns, grouped into two geographical divisions known as the Upper and Lower towns. Upper Creeks lived primarily along the Coosa and Tallapoosa River systems, while the Lower Creeks called the Chattahoochee and Flint watersheds home. Although these groups worked closely together on matters of shared political, economic, and cultural interests, profound divisions within Creek society over the issue of escalating American settlement in their homeland and mounting interference in traditional ways of life had begun to emerge by the first decade of the nineteenth century.[12]

Tecumseh. Courtesy of the Library of Congress.

The Creeks had long been courted by the Americans who jealously looked on their rich lands as well suited for large-scale agriculture. In the 1790s the United States government appointed agent Benjamin Hawkins to spearhead the United States government's effort to convince the Creeks to adopt tenets of American lifestyles, especially the undertaking of plow agriculture, in large part in the hope that they would as a consequence need less land to live on, and vast expanses of their former hunting grounds could therefore be opened to American settlement. The plan only highlighted growing divisions in Creek society. Those who embraced it, and its associated meddling in the affairs of Creek government, in effect were forced to reject their ancestral way of life while their kinsmen pursued a different course. The Federal Road became one of the most visible focal points of this escalating tension. A government-sponsored route through the heart of Creek territory, the road connected central Georgia with the small but growing American settlements north of Mobile. The road had been designed as a vital link in a road system that would ultimately connect the nation's capital with the port city of New Orleans. From the Creeks' point of view, it was nothing less than an unwelcome superhighway facilitating the invasion of their homeland by thousands of illegal white settlers.[13]

By 1811 the Creek Nation contained deep divisions among its people over what course of action to pursue. The visit of the Shawnee chief, Tecumseh, who traveled to the Mississippi Territory from the Great Lakes region, would become the proverbial spark that would help channel the growing spirit of resistance among a portion of the Creeks into direct action by transforming a political vision into a religious crusade. Assisted by his brother, Tenskwatawa (The Prophet), Tecumseh preached to all who would listen that an Indian Confederacy, returning to native traditions and eschewing all traces of American influence, was the only way to ensure the survival of native tribes in the face of mounting encroachment on their lands. In the summer and fall of 1811, he traveled throughout the Southeast in an attempt to rally Indian groups to his cause. He met with little success with all but a portion of the already receptive Upper Creeks, many of whom he addressed at the Creek annual council meeting at Tuckaubatchee. In the coming months, Red Sticks, so named for the red war clubs that symbolized their aggressive posture, began threatening Creek leaders who favored accommodation with the Americans and took to destroying livestock and other symbols of American-style agriculture. Soon a civil war among the Creeks erupted that threatened to engulf the entire Southwest in fiery conflict. Alarm spread throughout the Mississippi Territory. Just over a decade old and riddled with political and regional factionalism since its founding, American settlers throughout the isolated region for the first time began to galvanize to face a perceived common threat.[14]

Two

ALABAMA IN FLAMES

The Creek War and War of 1812

The Creek War and the closely related War of 1812 are watershed events in Alabama's development. The results of the conflicts forever broke the power of the Creek Nation, set a precedent for Indian Removal, opened much of the future state to American settlement, and brought to an end European control of any portion of the region.

Violence between Red Sticks and American settlers first flared up in the spring of 1812 in the form of isolated attacks within the Mississippi Territory and as far north as Tennessee. In accordance with Agent Benjamin Hawkins's orders that the instigators be apprehended, Creek leaders under his sway found and killed the culprits of some of the initial attacks. These actions only exacerbated tensions within the Creek Nation. Red Sticks, outraged at their fellow kinsmen for carrying out Hawkins's orders and steadily growing bolder and more determined in their plans, soon looked to the Spanish in Pensacola in an attempt to obtain additional arms as they prepared for a wider conflict. With open warfare seemingly inevitable, American officials in the Mississippi Territory began to mobilize forces to respond in case of emergency. Panicked settlers in the Tensaw-Tombigbee region constructed a

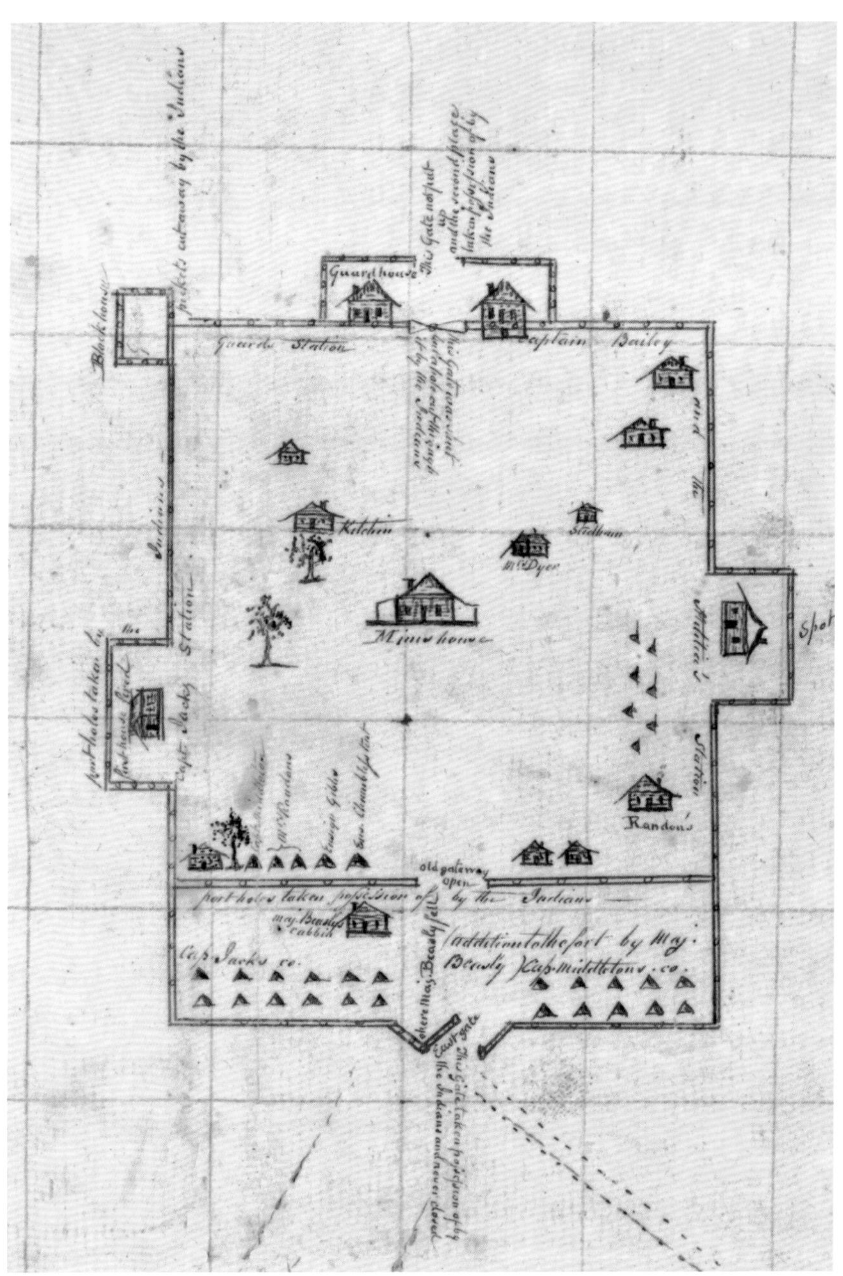

Sketch of Fort Mims, showing the location of structures within the compound. Courtesy of the Alabama Department of Archives and History.

series of makeshift stockades as places of temporary refuge should the escalating conflict become more general.[1]

The first battle of the Creek War took place near Burnt Corn Creek, in modern southwestern Alabama, as a result of local militia efforts to track down a group of Red Stick warriors that had attempted to secure arms and ammunition at Pensacola. Troops under Colonel James Caller found and attacked the Red Stick encampment on the morning of July 27, 1813. Caller's men initially scattered them in disorder. When the warriors rallied and counterattacked, however, the startled militiamen fled in terror. The victory gave the Red Sticks a newfound confidence in their martial abilities and caused more settlers across the region to flee to the perceived safety of their stockades. What happened next at one of them sent shock waves throughout the nation.[2]

Fort Mims was typical of the many settler stockades constructed in the region in that it had been built around several structures on the plantation of Samuel Mims. It featured split log walls, two gates, and a partially constructed blockhouse in addition to several outbuildings. By the end of August 1813, it held approximately 250 settlers, just over one hundred troops of the Mississippi Territorial militia, and about forty local militiamen under the overall command of Major Daniel Beasley. Because many of the fort's inhabitants were people of Creek ancestry who had not sided with the Red Sticks, it became the special target of a well-planned surprise attack overseen by mixed-blood chieftain William Weatherford.[3]

At noon on August 30, 1813, hundreds of Red Stick warriors, concealed in the woods near the fort, rose and ran silently toward it at the command of one of their leaders. They went unnoticed until within a few steps of the stockade and, the gate being open, took those inside by complete surprise. The occupants of Fort Mims were nearly overwhelmed and forced to flee to the interior structures of the fort to organize a defense. They at length managed to stem the initial Red Stick onslaught, but the attackers regrouped and launched a second assault later in the day, which spelled their doom. In this second assault the Red Sticks began to set fire to the structures inside the fort, and the garrison was gradually corralled into one bastion. In the massacre that followed, Fort Mims was destroyed and the majority of those in it were killed. Red Sticks brutally murdered and scalped hundreds of men, women, and children as the fighting wore on into the afternoon. Only a handful of those in the fort, no more than a few dozen, managed to make a desperate escape. Perhaps one hundred were captured.[4]

Depiction of the attack on Fort Mims, courtesy of the History Museum of Mobile. Early depictions of the Battle of Fort Mims commonly exaggerated the savage nature of the Creek warriors and played into perceptions the affair was an unprovoked attack on unsuspecting white settlers.

Fear spread throughout the Southwest frontier and beyond regarding what the strike portended for American settlements. Even as far away as Natchez, rumors ran wild that Native Americans targeted the area for attack. As reports circulated across the nation about what had happened at Mims, armies were raised within the Mississippi Territory, Georgia, and Tennessee to put down the rebellion.[5]

The Mississippi territorial militia, under the command of Ferdinand Claiborne, became the first army to be engaged as it scouted for Red Sticks in the lower Tombigbee and Alabama River areas in the weeks after the fall of Fort Mims. Some of these soldiers in November took part in one of the enduring legends of the Creek War. Aboard canoes in the Alabama River, Captain Sam Dale and two privates rowed by a black man named Caesar fought a dramatic hand-to-hand battle with a group of Red Stick warriors more than twice their number. In what became known as the Canoe Fight, Dale and his men used knives, bayonets, gun butts, and oars in a brief but desperate affair that resulted in a victory that greatly improved the morale of the American army. The Americans killed every one of the Red Stick warriors as fellow soldiers on the riverbank "kept up such interminable yell of encouragement that little else

Depiction of the Canoe Fight, from J. F. H. Claiborne's *The Life and Times of Sam Dale*. Courtesy of the Alabama Department of Archives and History.

could be heard." Despite the small numbers of participants, the audaciousness of the affair made Dale a national hero.[6]

Claiborne's army's ultimate target that fall and winter was the Red Stick stronghold at the village and spiritual center known as the Holy Ground. On December 23, 1813, his force of volunteers, militia, and friendly Choctaws arrived there and opened the attack. They steadily drove the Red Sticks back and in a short time forced a disorderly retreat that sent the defenders "flying in all directions, many of them casting away their arms." One of the last to retreat, noted chieftain William Weatherford, made a dramatic escape that has become engrained in myth. While under fire, he jumped his trusted horse, Arrow, off a high bluff into the river and in a hail of bullets disappeared into the forest on the opposite bank of the Alabama. The victors remained in the area only a short time before returning to their base of supply at Fort Claiborne. Another sortie into the Creek heartland via the Alabama and Cahaba Rivers, led by Colonel Gilbert C. Russell, launched from the fort early in 1814. The ill-fated expedition fell apart before fighting any major battles, however, as communication problems and logistical difficulties turned it into more of a fight for survival than a raid into enemy territory.[7]

Depiction of the Battle of Autossee. Courtesy of the Hargrett Rare Book and Manuscript Library / University of Georgia Libraries.

Two other armies, raised by the state of Georgia, arrived in the region in the fall of 1813. The smaller of the two forces, under General David Adams, advanced on the Tallapoosa in December 1813. Finding only empty villages, it did not become engaged in any major battles though it did skirmish with Red Sticks during its advance and retreat. General John Floyd commanded the larger Georgia army raised in response to the Red Stick threat. On arrival at the Chattahoochee River from central Georgia, where he had come to relieve a Red Stick siege of the allied Creek town of Coweta, Floyd's men constructed Fort Mitchell to serve as a base of supply.[8]

Floyd ended up making two serious offensives into the heart of Creek territory. The first ended on the frosty morning of November 29, 1813, at the village of Autossee, a significant Red Stick population center on the Tallapoosa. In a pitched battle, Floyd's men shot down approximately two hundred Red Sticks and destroyed the village. Floyd could not immediately follow up on his stunning victory due to logistical issues associated with keeping the army supplied in its advanced position, though, and retraced his steps to Fort Mitchell to regroup. The army took the field again in January 1814. As it paused to camp

General Andrew Jackson. Courtesy of the Library of Congress.

near a tributary of the Tallapoosa known as Calabee Creek, it fell victim to one of the best-planned Red Stick assaults of the war. Just before dawn on January 27, 1814, over one thousand warriors fell on Floyd's unsuspecting army and nearly overwhelmed the American position. In desperate fighting, in which Floyd's Yuchi allies played a key role, the army at length slowed the Red Stick onslaught and drove off the attackers. With his army weakened and his troops' terms of enlistment about to expire, though, Floyd could not advance and marched the majority of his men back to Georgia.[9]

The most famous of the campaigns of the Creek War, conducted by Tennessee soldiers led by Andrew Jackson, sealed the fate of the Red Stick rebellion. Jackson was given command of one of two forces of Tennessee militia raised in response to the attack on Fort Mims as well as a large cavalry unit under the leadership of his trusted friend and confidant John Coffee. A force from East Tennessee under General John Cocke was to cooperate with Jackson's command.[10]

The Tennesseans marched south into the Mississippi Territory in the fall of 1813 and immediately set about their work with cruel efficiency. On November 3, 1813, Coffee's men surrounded and destroyed the town of Tallushatchee in what is remembered as more of a massacre than a battle. In only thirty minutes, Coffee's troops killed almost two hundred Red Sticks, causing Tennessee volunteer David Crockett to remark afterward that "we shot them like dogs." Shortly thereafter, Jackson received a plea for help from the nearby friendly Creek village of Talladega, which found itself besieged by Red Sticks. On November 9, 1813, using the same plan that Coffee had used at Tallushatchee, Jackson attempted to encircle and destroy the town. Jackson's men shot down the Red Sticks in droves in the battle, but a failure to complete the envelopment allowed hundreds to escape. Nonetheless, within the span of a week Americans had won two smashing victories in this theater of the war and seriously weakened the Red Sticks' strength.[11]

Jackson could not take to the field again until January 1814 because of delays owing to struggles in keeping his largely volunteer army supplied and intact. This time he targeted Tohopeka, a village in a horseshoe-shaped curve of the Tallapoosa River where a large Red Stick force had gathered. The village and a large number of warriors lay behind an elaborate wooden barricade stretching across the top of the "horseshoe." As Jackson's men approached Tohopeka, however, they became entangled in two surprise attacks that forced Jackson to abandon this first attempt to reduce the stronghold. On January 22, 1814, Red Sticks attacked Jackson at Emuckfau Creek, a few miles from the fortification. Two days later, on January 24, the Red Sticks attacked again as the army crossed Enitachopco Creek. At length driving off the attackers in close-quarters affairs that could have easily wrecked Jackson's army, the men had little choice but to retreat and regroup.[12]

After receiving reinforcements a short time later, which swelled his army to over five thousand men, Jackson set out again for Tohopeka. He arrived on March 27, 1814, to find over one thousand warriors under the Red Stick leader Menawa awaiting him behind an impressive fortification. Jackson deemed the barricade one of the best-planned defensive positions he had ever seen. He opened the Battle of Horseshoe Bend at 10:30 A.M. with an artillery bombardment, hoping to weaken the Red Stick defenses. As the Red Sticks screamed defiance, his artillery ineffectually poured shots into their stout fortification. During the bombardment, several Cherokee allies under Coffee crossed the river behind the village and captured the Red Sticks' canoes to prevent them from being used to escape. They then pressed on into the village and succeeded in setting several of its structures on fire. When Jackson saw the smoke from these fires, he ordered an all-out frontal assault. His soldiers charged energetically and scaled the fortifications in a matter of minutes in some of the most

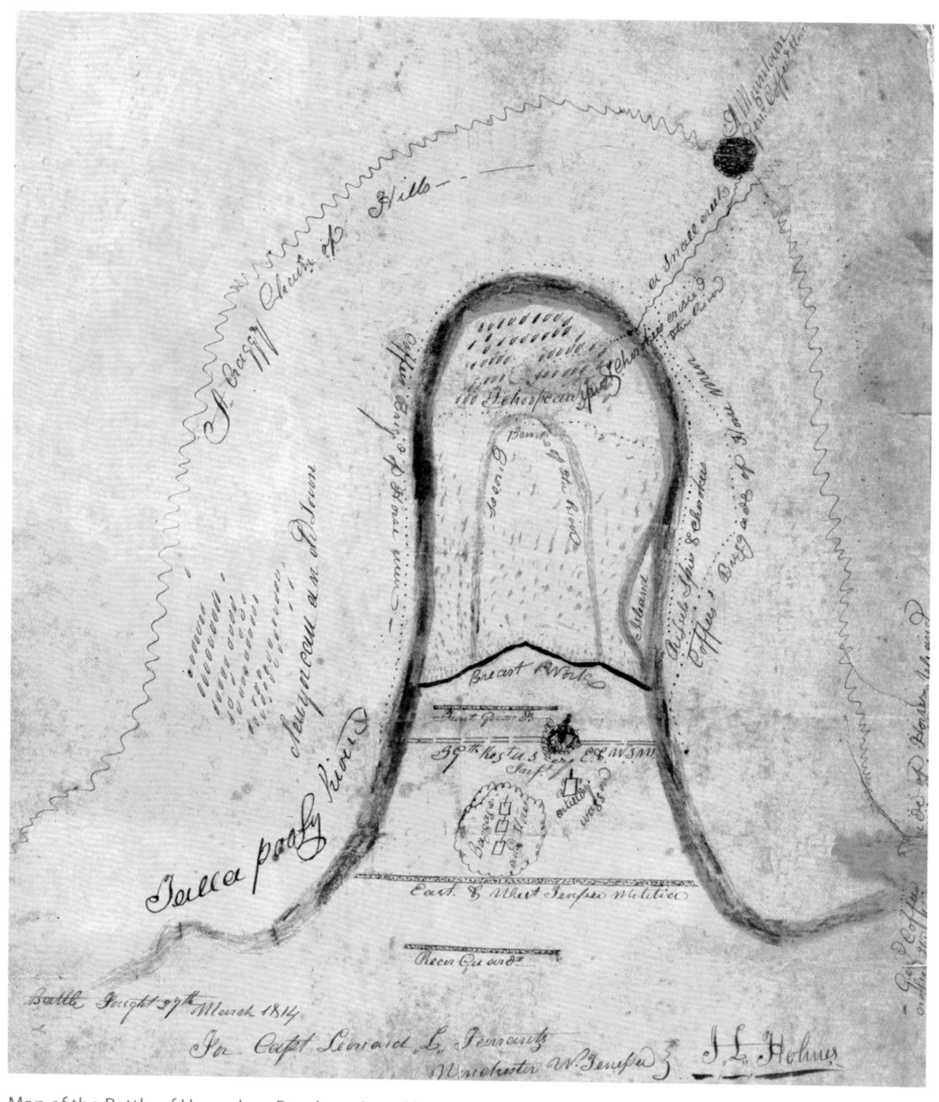

Map of the Battle of Horseshoe Bend produced by Leonard Tarrant. Courtesy of the Alabama Department of Archives and History.

brutal combat to take place during the entire war. The Red Sticks resisted valiantly, but once their barricade had been breached, the battle turned into a prolonged slaughter in which more Indians would die than in any other battle in the history of the United States. Jackson's men counted over 550 Red Stick bodies on the field after the battle, and officers estimated the total killed to be upwards of nine hundred. The Red Stick army had been shattered.[13]

Jackson did not know the extent of his triumph at the time, however, and next targeted an area known as the Hickory Ground at the confluence of the Coosa and Tallapoosa Rivers. After constructing Fort Jackson there on the site of an earlier French fort built a century earlier, he received hundreds of starving Creek refugees, many of them allies, who began making their way into the army's encampment. Even the principal Red Stick leader, William Weatherford, bravely entered the camp and surrendered to Jackson, claiming he had no more warriors with which to fight him. Amazed by his courage, Jackson spared him on the promise that he would urge other warriors to likewise lay down their arms. As refugees continued to pour into the camp, it soon became obvious to all that the war was indeed over.[14]

General Thomas Pinckney and Creek Indian agent Benjamin Hawkins were assigned to draft a peace treaty with the Creeks in the aftermath of the dissolution of the Red Sticks as a fighting force. Jackson triumphantly returned to Tennessee in the meantime, feted along the way at places such as Huntsville as a conquering hero. But shortly after his return to Nashville he received a promotion to the rank of major general and assumed command of the Seventh Military District, in which the primary theater of action of the Creek War lay. He promptly returned to the area to assume control of the treaty negotiations himself. Jackson exacted an incredible toll from the Creeks, both allied with and hostile to the Americans. In the end he demanded the cession of over twenty million acres of land, almost one-half of all Creek territory, to the United States and the removal of the area's native inhabitants to the shrunken remainder of their lands. They protested to the degree they could, but the Creeks had little choice but to sign the Treaty of Fort Jackson on August 9, 1814.[15]

The ink had not yet dried on the treaty when the larger War of 1812 took center stage in the region. Jackson already knew of British plans for an offensive somewhere along the Gulf Coast. In May 1814, British forces had landed on the coast of Florida and set up a post along the Apalachicola River as a base from which to recruit Red Stick Creeks as allies in a planned southern campaign along the Gulf Coast. Had they arrived earlier, their efforts might have seriously threatened American armies in the region. By the time British plans got underway, however, the Red Sticks had suffered the devastating defeat at Horseshoe Bend and their power as a fighting force had been shattered. In late August, Jackson moved his headquarters to Mobile, closer to the developing threat, and began strengthening Fort Bowyer on Mobile Point in order to better guard against any attempt by the British to enter Mobile Bay. The city and surrounding region had only recently come under American control, seized

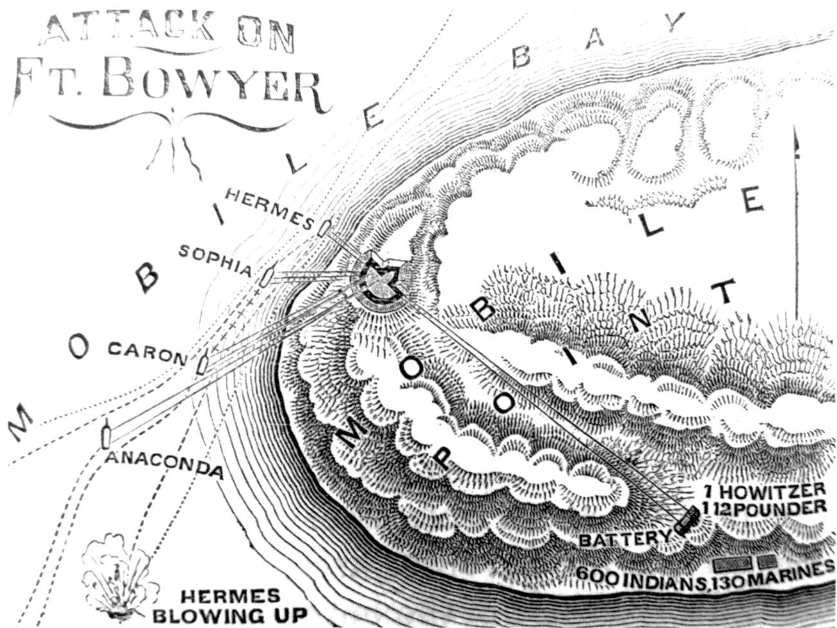

Map of the attack on Fort Bowyer in September 1814. Courtesy of the Historic New Orleans Collection.

from the Spanish by General James Wilkinson in April 1813. On September 12, 1814, British soldiers and allied Indians landed near Fort Bowyer to assault it from the rear, while a small naval squadron moved into position to bombard it simultaneously from the sea. The outnumbered American defenders managed to repel both the land and naval forces and so severely damage the frigate *Hermes* that it had to be destroyed. The British limped ignominiously back to Pensacola, which they had earlier established as their base of operations, in the aftermath of the failed assault to rethink their plan of attack.[16]

Jackson seized the initiative in the interlude by launching a campaign from Mobile to prevent the British from further using the valuable Spanish port. He secured the surrender of Pensacola on November 7, 1814, and then moved to head off the British at New Orleans once it at length became clear they would next target the Crescent City. There on a plain along the Mississippi on January 8, 1815, he won the famed Battle of New Orleans in one of the most lopsided victories in the annals of America's military history. Frustrated but undeterred, the British retreated back down the Mississippi and undertook a second attempt to capture Mobile in order to approach New Orleans overland. This time more than six hundred troops supported by a sizable force of artillery went ashore to attack Fort Bowyer by land while British ships prepared for a bombardment from the sea. American commander William Lawrence recognized the hopelessness of his position at a glance and surrendered on February 11. British preparations for capturing Mobile and continuing their advance were well underway when word of the Treaty of Ghent, signed months earlier in Belgium and ending the war, at last arrived. A defining period of turmoil in Alabama's territorial history ended when the guns fell silent. A new era of unprecedented development was about to begin.[17]

ALABAMA FEVER

The Great Migration

With the opening of millions of acres of its lands to Americans as a result of the Creek War, Alabama became the centerpiece destination of a massive westward migration. The rapid pace of settlement defined the final years of its territorial experience and laid the foundation for its development as a state.

A sudden, massive immigration is one of the enduring hallmarks of Alabama's territorial experience and a fundamental component of its formative era. While both western and eastern sections of the Mississippi Territory welcomed an influx of settlers after the Creek War, the pace of settlement became especially rapid in what would become Alabama. The "Alabama country" beckoned settlers by flaunting millions of acres of some of the richest land the country could offer. Its most fertile stretches enthralled new arrivals as a land of opportunity. Exceptionally well suited for agriculture—especially the production of the most lucrative cash crop of the era, cotton—they viewed it as an agricultural paradise. The land boasted a long growing season, abundant rainfall, numerous navigable streams, and a mild climate. Newspapers, travelers' guides, and personal correspondence glowingly described the territory as a sort of modern Eden for its natural

The Tennessee River at Florence. Photograph by Mike Bunn.

abundance, and observers as far away as New York pronounced the territory an "American Canaan."[1]

A startled North Carolinian described the infatuation with the new land in blunt fashion and inadvertently gave an enduring name to the wanderlust the region's luxuriance inspired. "The *Alabama Feaver* [*sic*] rages here with great violence and has *carried off* vast numbers of our citizens," he wrote to a friend in 1817. "There is no question that this feaver is contagious . . . for as soon as one neighbor visits another who has just returned from the Alabama he immediately discovers the same symptoms which are exhibited by the person who has seen the allureing [*sic*] Alabama."[2]

In truth the eastern section of the Mississippi Territory emerged for a time as the epicenter of a westward movement from America's eastern seaboard to its southwestern frontier termed by historians the Great Migration. In 1800 only two American states existed west of the Appalachian mountains, with a combined population of under four hundred thousand people. By 1820, eight new states had been formed in the American Southwest, which collectively claimed over two million residents. Alabama's growth in this era proved especially dramatic. Just before the War of 1812 the area that became the state of Mississippi claimed over three times the American population of the future state of Alabama; some thirty-one thousand residents compared to barely nine thousand. By the end of the ensuing decade Alabama could boast of nearly 150,000 free and enslaved residents—an astounding sixteenfold increase—while Mississippi could claim a respectable seventy-five thousand. This peopling of Alabama was general but uneven, as the first settlers concentrated within fertile river valleys and the areas of richer soils in the Tennessee River Valley region, a wide arc stretching through the central sections of the state, and its well-watered

Drawing of a stagecoach, which appeared in Basil Hall's *Forty Etchings: From Sketches Made with the Camera Lucida, in North America, in 1827 and 1828*. Courtesy of the Columbus Museum.

southwestern section. All this migratory movement filled the region's few roads with incredible activity. One traveler along the Federal Road in Georgia in 1816 reported seeing in the course of a little over a week an incredible 141 wagons, 102 carts, 10 stagecoaches, 14 gigs, 29 droves of cattle, 27 droves of hogs, 2 droves of sheep, and some 3,840 people—all bound for Alabama.[3]

"By horse, by wagon, by boat, and by foot the flood of humanity poured in," observed one historian of this mass movement. Most of them traveled in groups for safety and comradery, often with several families from the same vicinity making the trip together. Their departures were marked with heart-rending goodbyes to other loved ones they knew they might never see again and were filled with the anxiety, upheaval, and uncertainty that naturally accompanied a move from an established homeplace to an undeveloped frontier. For many of them, the trip was a very long one of several hundred miles along poorly maintained trails through the wilderness. For a smaller number, the trip involved merely crossing the Georgia or Tennessee border or floating down one of the region's major waterways to their destination or sailing into its primary port at Mobile and thence upriver. They traveled with everything they owned packed up in wagons, carts, trunks, and in hogshead barrels, and whatever cattle and hogs they possessed were driven along the road with them. A small number occasionally stopped for the evening at one of the few roadside taverns in the region, but for the overwhelming majority, the only stops were to make nightly camps where they cooked whatever food they had and gathered around the fire for warmth and conversation before getting some sleep under the stars.[4]

Travelers usually departed in the fall when the weather was more comfortable, roads were generally in their best condition, and the numerous swift-flowing creeks and rivers that needed to be crossed were less susceptible to sudden flooding. Advancing perhaps ten to twenty-five miles per day, the journey often involved a few weeks of travel at minimum and for many a month or more.[5]

The overwhelming majority of most of these early Alabama settlers are remembered in history as statistics, their migration recorded in census records, charts, and tables that merely demonstrate their presence. The experiences of a few have been rescued from obscurity by genealogists searching for their ancestors or historical societies seeking to communicate the facts about the roots of some of the communities they founded or the circumstances of the construction of the few structures they built that survive to this day. The truth is that we have documentation of the travails and triumphs of an exceedingly small number of early Alabama settlers, and we must rely on them to illuminate and give color to those of their multitudinous peers.

The story of John Hunt, founder and namesake of Huntsville, is one of those better-known migration stories from which we can extrapolate much information that helps us understand the context of his journey, arrival, and life in territorial Alabama. Hunt had been born in Virginia about 1750 and, having moved to North Carolina as a teen, rose to some prominence there. He became a county sheriff and later a captain of militia in North Carolina's western region—what became Tennessee—in its territorial days. While he and his family lived moderately well in the east Tennessee mountain country for over a decade in the 1790s and early 1800s, the type of fortune he sought eluded him. Restlessly casting about for a more promising locale, when he heard rumblings about the opening of rich Cherokee land in the northern portion of the Mississippi Territory he became among the first to explore it. He, like so many others throughout Alabama's early history, determined to settle there after a brief reconnaissance and claim his land by preemption once it could be surveyed and sold.[6]

Hunt staked out his claim to a portion of a lush valley north of the Tennessee River watered by a large spring overlooked by a scenic bluff; a promising spot that today is the heart of downtown Huntsville. He returned to Tennessee to pack up his family and prepare for the move. On his journey back, several members of at least one, and possibly more, neighboring families, intrigued with what Hunt described and likewise seeking a new start in a more lucrative location, accompanied him. These early arrivals found ample game, fertile soil, good water, and a hospitable climate. Soon others came to live nearby, drawn by these same assets and motivated for the journey by the same pursuit of prosperity. Thus, from a simple cluster of cabins and small homesteads one of early Alabama's most important population and trading centers quickly arose.[7]

Hunt's saga is informative and illuminating and in some ways is the prototypical territorial community development story. Since, except as oral legend, little of it comes from Hunt's own hand; however, it lacks the visceral immediacy of tales of immigration written by travelers themselves. We are fortunate to have access to a few accounts of migrations, which help us understand the experience on an individual level. Margaret Ervin Austill, for example, made the trip from Georgia to the Mississippi Territory as a young girl in the spring of 1811 as part of a large group of "about one hundred slaves, men, women and children" from three families. She remembered the poignant "weeping at parting from dear old friends" that accompanied their departure as well as the wry toast her aunt gave her father and uncle as they left, expressing her hope that they would be blessed with good luck but sure that "the next thing I hear will be that you all have been scalped by the savages." Margaret's family made their journey as part of the first wave of immigration to what is now Alabama, prior to the Creek War, during a time of rising tensions with the region's Native American population. "We were joined by many movers, which gave us more security," she remembered. "At night the wagons were all fixed round the encampment, the women and children and negroes in the center, the men keeping guard with guns, so we made a formidable appearance of defense." The group stopped in Clarke County expecting to grow a crop of corn with

Henry Hitchcock, taken from *The Genealogy of the Hitchcock Family: Who Are Descended from Matthias Hitchcock of East Haven, Conn., and Luke Hitchcock of Wethersfield, Conn.* By Rev. Dwight D. Marsh (Amherst, MA: Carpenter and Morehouse, 1894).

which to restore their teams before continuing the exhausting journey west, and Margaret recalled seeing slaves with a whipsaw prepare the lumber for the cabins they temporarily were to call home. After the corn had been gathered many of this little band of settlers decided to stay, however. In the words of her father, which Margaret overheard in a conversation with his brother, "the water is splendid, the land good enough, and you have made a fine crop of corn, we have wild game plenty for the shooting, and I can't see that we could do better."[8]

Others experienced a much less pleasant arrival in Alabama. Creek War veteran Richard Breckinridge became one of hundreds of the soldiers from that war to consider moving south from his native Tennessee after discovering the richness of the area's lands. While on a trip in 1816 to scout out a spot to settle, he accidentally cut his foot while chopping wood for a campfire and suddenly found himself in a very dangerous situation. Severely wounded and in the middle of an unfamiliar wilderness, he managed to make his way to an Indian's cabin he remembered passing earlier on his journey. The man kindly helped him recover enough to continue his trip. He proceeded alone in the heat of summer through some of the most sparsely settled portions of the territory, through what is now northwestern Alabama and into the area of modern Jefferson County. He is lucky to have survived. "I am in a great anxiety," he recorded in his journal a week into his adventure. "This is the fifth day that I have seen neither Indian nor white man." With his foot showing signs of infection and his horse hobbled from an arduous journey through briar-choked thickets and steep, rocky terrain, he searched frantically for a major river he could follow in hopes of finding a settlement. Rain pelted him several times as he traveled, ticks and rattlesnakes beset his path, and mosquitoes tormented him as he attempted to sleep. Suffering from hunger and thirst, he at length stumbled into the young settlements in Jones Valley (modern greater Birmingham) where he managed to buy meal and buttermilk from a miller and learned a great deal about the rich river region to the south. He made his way home soon after, gathered his family, and returned to settle along the Tombigbee in the Alabama Territory.[9]

Even though he migrated directly to one of Alabama's largest cities, on his arrival in January 1817, Henry Hitchcock perceived himself in a wilderness every bit as untamed as the one through which Breckinridge struggled. Hitchcock, the grandson of Revolutionary War hero Ethan Allen, left his native Vermont and a promising legal career there for opportunity in the rapidly growing Southwest. He began his journey in the fall of 1816 and traveled through New York and Philadelphia before taking a ride on a flatboat at Pittsburgh down the Ohio and Mississippi. To help offset the price of his passage, he even manned the oars himself at stretches. Hitchcock disembarked at Natchez and after a quick survey of the prospects there, a community already flooded with lawyers, determined to strike out for Mobile. He judged his new home as remote by any standard, describing it unflatteringly in a letter to a friend as "200 miles from civilization, surrounded by Indians," and "isolated from the world." He found the signs of growth all around him encouraging, nonetheless, and decided to open a law practice in the port city. In hindsight the move may have been one of desperation as much as foresight—according to legend he arrived in town with a mere twenty-five cents in his pocket and needed to earn money quickly. He had to wait two months before his first client walked through the door, but within a year he had managed to open a partnership in the nearby territorial capital of Saint Stephens and buy a house there for himself and his family. Rising from obscurity to prominence in short order, he won appointment as secretary of the territory in 1818 and would soon become one of the most influential men in early Alabama's political scene.[10]

Gideon Lincecum's migration to the Alabama Territory from Georgia in 1818 as a part of a group of about twenty-five family members and slaves was more typical of the immigrant experience. Lincecum's father, like so many others, had scouted portions of the land prior to the move and determined it rich and promising enough to make it his family's new home despite its small population. "Altogether, it was the wildest, least-trodden and tomahawk-marked country he had ever explored, and the soil was rich enough," Lincecum remembered. Lincecum reveled in the family's trek through an "unhacked forest," likening the trip to "a big camp hunt." Indeed, his account of their journey west reads as early American high adventure: the caravan crossed unbridged watercourses; gathered wild fruits and nuts; fished numerous streams; and hunted deer, turkey, ducks and wild pigeons, which they cooked in their nightly camp. He estimated they traveled about five hundred miles over a period of about six weeks, proclaiming the entire journey to be "delightful beyond description." Lincecum at length reached the "small log cabin village" of Tuscaloosa and determined to settle there while his father and other family members moved farther downriver. They raised corn, hunted bear and deer, and fished, but found obtaining provisions they could not raise themselves, such as flour, sugar, and coffee, enormously expensive. He had just built a "little clapboard house on the river side of the town," when his father visited him and told him he had found an even more desirable tract of land farther west along the Tombigbee. Soon the entire group was again on the road.[11]

Indeed, many of Alabama's early American settlers, in similar fashion to Lincecum, continued their migration after arrival. Early observers of the people of Alabama, including missionaries, travelers, and settlers themselves, often remarked how "many of the persons now there are not stationary." Some new arrivals moved elsewhere in the state after a short sojourn in the first place they stopped, but many continued farther westward, on as far as Texas and Missouri, constantly in search of better land, more promising opportunities, and just the right situation. In one of the few studies of residency in the period, Tennessee Valley historian Daniel S. Dupre found that a mere 16 percent of over two hundred heads of household he sampled from an 1815 tax list in

Madison County were still there in 1830. The pure love of moving sparked some of the apparent restlessness. On asking why one family he encountered had chosen to abandon a spot they had improved for an unknown plot elsewhere, a contemporary observer received the deadpan reply that they had been "doing so all our lives, just moving from place to place—never resting. As soon as ever we get comfortably settled, then it is time to be off to something new."[12]

The majority of these new arrivals hailed from other, older southern states. From the north came Tennesseans and Kentuckians, while from the east came Georgians, North and South Carolinians, and even a few Virginians. There were even a few genuine Yankees among the first generation of Alabama settlers as well, for small numbers of native New Englanders could be found in every corner of the future state; they played a significant role in founding some of its earliest communities. While most of the new immigrants arrived from elsewhere in America, a substantial number came from Europe. These "old world" settlers, who came primarily from the British Isles with a smattering of French and Germans among their numbers, often were fleeing the same sort of difficult economic conditions as their American-born neighbors and similarly were hoping to find their fortune in the area's rich soil. In a curious turn of events that resulted in one of the enduring legends of Alabama's territorial period, a small band of exiled veterans of Napoleon's defeated army and French refugees from a slave rebellion in Saint Domingue (Haiti) made their way to what is now Marengo County beginning in 1817 at the invitation of the federal government. The group had been awarded over ninety thousand acres of prime land along the Tombigbee in hopes they would create a new bastion of frontier settlement. As the scheme called for the new immigrants to support themselves through the cultivation of grapes and olives, it is remembered as the Vine and Olive Colony. Between one hundred and two hundred people established the town of Demopolis on the granted lands, only to discover their initial start at a settlement lay outside the tract they had been given. The new town they subsequently attempted to create a short distance away within the bounds of their allotment, Aigleville, proved stillborn. Owing in part to this inauspicious effort at town-building as well as the agricultural underpinning of the settlement's planned economy, the French community that developed in the area appeared even at its height more an agrarian enclave than urban center. Even if they found the physical appearance of the fledgling colony unremarkable, visitors noted the founders' unmistakable pride in their ancestry and robust hospitality. During his visit there, George S. Gaines reported that he dined on good French food and wine and stayed in a cabin adorned with

Depiction of the Vine and Olive Colony. Courtesy of the Alabama Department of Archives and History.

a large French flag and others captured on the battlefields of Europe. A bust of Napoleon sat on a cedar block in one corner of a room, while on a table sat a "fine silver mounted travelling case with silver items—a gift from the Emperor himself." The colony never developed as envisioned, however. Many of the grantees never even set foot on their allotments, and those who did had to battle an unfamiliar and unforgiving climate, among other obstacles, in attempting to create profitable enterprises. In the end, other, more lucrative, opportunities in places such as Texas, New Orleans, Mobile, and elsewhere lured away many settlers and hastened the end of the effort before it really got started. Within less than two decades, most of the French immigrants who had attempted to settle in central Alabama had departed the area for various reasons. The few remaining could be found scattered on various small farmsteads throughout the area.[13]

For most early settlers, obtaining legal title to the land they claimed, improved, and supplied themselves from proved more complicated than accepting a grant, as the French-Haitian refugees had done. Most of the territory in which all these settlers arrived lay within the federal domain only recently acquired via cession from native groups. Other sections languished in a tangle of overlapping patents issued by various European authorities. Throughout the limits of both, squatters gathered in hopes of being granted

preemption at best or being in position to buy their claim in time at worst. Many were technically subject to eviction since the land they occupied had not been surveyed and offered for sale yet, but such measures were rarely enforced. Judge Harry Toulmin lamented the situation by asking a rhetorical question explaining the dilemma in administering justice: "How can a jury be found in Monroe County to convict a man of intrusion—where every man is an intruder." Surveyors such as the capable Thomas Freeman, a friend of George Washington who had helped lay out the nation's capital, would in time divide the territory into many sections, ranges, and townships. The subsequent free-for-all of legal land buying in Alabama began in earnest the latter half of 1817 at offices including Milledgeville, Georgia, Saint Stephens, and Huntsville, and the exchange of notes and money soon reached a fever pitch. Purchases of large tracts of thousands of acres were not unusual, especially in the rich river bottomlands prized by the first wave of Alabama planters. For the most part, though, the territory would be settled in much smaller plots purchased in fractional sections at the rate of as little as two dollars per acre with a nominal amount of cash down and the remainder due over a period of years.[14]

It is illustrative of the type of society in which Alabama developed that almost half of all of those arriving during its territorial and early statehood years could trace their lineage to Africa. Slaves of course had no choice in

A slave coffle on the road. Courtesy of the Library of Congress.

their emigration, whether they came walking over wilderness roads from the Upper South with the families for whom they toiled or forcibly marched in coffles or shipped to the area so that they could be placed on the nation's most rapidly expanding chattel labor market through regional dealers in places such as Natchez, New Orleans, and even Mobile. Slavery had already become deeply imprinted in American economic life in the first decades of the nineteenth century, and the opening of enormous swaths of some of the nation's best cotton lands in its southwestern region only accelerated its entrenchment. The growth of the slave population in Alabama proved to be nothing short of spectacular. In 1810 a mere 2,624 slaves resided in the three counties already formed in the section of the Mississippi Territory that eventually became the state of Alabama. By 1820 the slave population stood at over forty thousand individuals, approximately a third of all residents. The slave population would top one hundred thousand by 1830, and by the time of the Civil War in 1861 would approach half a million people and account for nearly half of the entire population of the state.[15]

Much like other aspects of Alabama society that first took root in the territorial and early statehood years, the contours of the institution of slavery were established in the period. In most regards they differed only by scale with those of the height of the antebellum era. We have a great deal more information about the lives of slaves during the later antebellum years when more and larger plantations were in operation across the South, generating exponentially more documentation and observation of bondsmen than those of its frontier days. The findings of studies of the slave community in the South in general, though, are applicable to early Alabama. The slave workday commonly began at or before daylight and ended at dusk. Everyone had a task; adults performed all manner of chores on small farms and plantations, such as clearing fields, planting, hoeing, gathering crops, cutting firewood and fence rails, and tending livestock, while children might be charged with carrying water to older slaves in the fields, and elderly slaves might help prepare food. Slaves customarily labored for their masters six days a week, with Sunday as the day off and sometimes Saturday being a half day. Depending on each master's prerogative, a few holidays might allow for all work to be halted; Christmas Day was observed almost universally, and at some places Independence Day and New Year's Day were observed as well. Except for the small number of slaves expected to work within the plantation house or employed at jobs such as carriage drivers and other more public duties, slaves wore clothing made of coarse, durable fabrics such as osnaburg and linsey-woolsey. Food was, in general, abundant but not varied, with rations of corn meal, salt pork, and molasses ubiquitous and flour, rice, peas, meal, and on occasion other meats added to the diet as they became available. There were, of course, many variations in this, depending on location and season. This often-monotonous fare could sometimes be supplemented with the produce from small vegetable plots and perhaps the meat of a few chickens, which masters often allowed slaves to tend for themselves, as well as the occasional fish, opossum, rabbit, squirrel, or other small game obtained in the nearby woods in their limited free time. Slaves almost invariably lived in humble, sparsely furnished wooden cabins, often featuring dirt floors. What limited medical care, such as it was, they received usually came from masters but sometimes from local physicians who might make periodic visits to area plantations.[16]

Slaves expressed their autonomy and discontent with their condition in a variety of ways, few more obvious than running away. It is difficult, in fact,

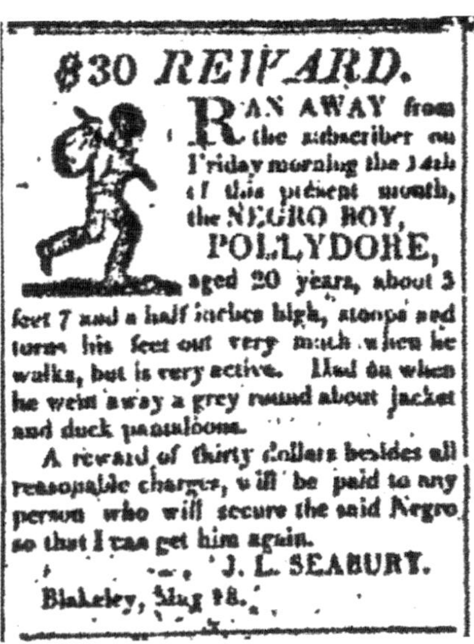

$30 REWARD.

RAN AWAY from the subscriber on Friday morning the 14th of this present month, the NEGRO BOY,

POLLYDORE,

aged 20 years, about 5 feet 7 and a half inches high, stoops and turns his feet out very much when he walks, but is very active. Had on when he went away a grey round about jacket and duck pantaloons.

A reward of thirty dollars besides all reasonable charges, will be paid to any person who will secure the said Negro so that I can get him again.

J. L. SEABURY.

Blakeley, Aug 18.

Runaway slave advertisement from the *Blakeley Sun*, 1819. Courtesy of Historic Blakeley State Park.

to find any issue of a major newspaper in Alabama's early statehood years that does not mention runaway slaves. The great majority were soon captured, having been tracked down with dogs, spotted by those seeking them, or betrayed by someone they came in contact with in their flight. Some simply returned of their own volition after coming to grips with the enormity of the task of truly finding freedom, or perhaps willing to face the consequences of their actions in return for a brief taste of independence. Slaves managed to find the greatest degree of dignity and self-determination in familial relations, both natural and fictive. Even for people granted as little agency as possible in the way they lived their lives, the concept of family remained a vital organizing and validating force and helped make a hopeless plight more bearable to some degree. Natural nuclear slave families did exist on farms and plantations, sometimes at the encouragement of masters, but owners as a rule viewed slave families as consisting of only a mother and children and proved all too willing to separate even these groups if financial considerations made it expedient. Slaves recognized aunts, uncles, and other extended kin either by blood or proximity, creating a community within a community that promoted a sense of belonging and fostered a social network that gave a degree of stability and control utterly lacking outside of the slave quarters.[17]

Deep-seated and abiding fear lay at the heart of the administration of the institution of slavery in early Alabama. Regardless of what masters might have said publicly or wanted to believe about the nature of the system of human bondage in which they engaged, they knew slaves were not happy with their lot. Tellingly, they recognized, and in some ways even exaggerated, their potential to work together to rebel. Even during Alabama's days as part of the sparsely populated Mississippi Territory, Governor David Holmes had confided in a letter how "scarcely a day passes without my receiving some information relative to the designs of those people (slaves) to insurrect." The frequency of such suspicions only grew as the number of slaves in the territory and state increased and events elsewhere stoked the fire of hysteria. Masters were keenly aware of famous slave rebellions such as the German Coast Uprising near New Orleans (1811), and later, the plot by Denmark Vesey in Charleston (1822), as well as a host of other smaller rumored rebellions throughout the region. Owners attempted to monitor and proscribe almost every activity by their slaves off the plantation grounds as a preventive measure against escape or insurrection, codifying an elaborate series of laws meant to help facilitate control. Alabama's constitution guaranteed the right of citizens to own slaves but outlined a compulsory patrol system, demanded that slaves traveling off their home plantation have a pass from their master, and outlined restrictions on slave gatherings. In general, prescriptions and suspicion progressively increased as time wore on in antebellum Alabama. In the state's first law-making session in 1819, for example, the Alabama legislature manumitted some seventeen slaves through an established legal process. Within just a few decades, manumission would become almost impossible in the state.[18]

The institution of slavery would become inextricably intertwined with early Alabama's economy due specifically to the rise of cotton production. Large-scale cotton production in Alabama dates to the territorial years and grew ever more important to its economy thereafter throughout the antebellum period. A glance at the steady rise in the number of bales shipped from the port of Mobile in early statehood illustrates its rise as Alabama's primary crop. In 1818 the port exported some seven thousand bales; ten thousand in 1819; sixteen thousand in 1820; twenty-five thousand in 1821; forty-five thousand in 1822, forty-nine thousand in 1823; forty-four thousand in 1824, and fifty-eight thousand in 1825. The trend continued almost unabated in the decades prior to the Civil War, so that by the 1850s, cotton production exceeded a staggering five hundred thousand bales per year in the state, the lion's share being sent to world markets via its gulf outlet. Yeomen farmers in every corner of early Alabama could be found harvesting small plots of cotton throughout the era, but cotton's position at the heart of Alabama's economy rested squarely on the backs of the enslaved. Slaves on Alabama's cotton plantations often devoted much of their labor throughout the year to cotton production. In February they plowed the fields, and planting began in March. They weeded and thinned the crop throughout the spring and summer and began picking bolls from the time they first began to open in August well into winter. Bondsmen were expected to pick staggering amounts of the fiber daily on the larger plantations—often as much as two hundred pounds in backbreaking work undertaken in all types of weather. They also performed most of the labor involved in its ginning, baling, and shipping.[19]

The maturation of Alabama's cotton economy lay years in advance of the entrance of the first American settlers in the territorial period. Yet, as with so many other aspects of the state's development, it had its origins in a tumultuous founding era that witnessed a wave of immigration bringing people and ideas about how to structure a society. Both would leave a deep and enduring impression on the state's legacy.

Four
ALABAMA
The Place and the People

The people who settled in Alabama during its territorial and early statehood years lived in a world shaped by a profound connection to the area's rich soil and a rugged independence born of necessity. Through the establishment of their farms and communities in an era of promising expansion, they gave birth to the society from which Alabama traces its origins.

Alabama's early American residents lived and labored in a place blessed with natural abundance. Thick primeval forests, brilliant green in summer and ablaze with color in autumn, dominated huge swaths of Alabama's landscape, their luxuriant growth inspiring awe in early arrivals and visitors. Rich riverside bottomlands featured incredible varieties of flora and fauna, while gently rolling hills and scattered prairies offered pristine vistas of an extremely fertile land that had, with few exceptions, never before been plowed. The land abounded with game. Deer, rabbits, turkeys, and squirrels were plentiful, and huge flocks of birds darkened the skies. Fish innumerable swam the clear waters of mighty rivers and the murmuring streams pulsing through the landscape. Several large predators, many now long vanished from most sections of the state, stalked its remotest reaches in significant numbers. The eerie glow of wolves' eyes twinkled in the firelight of nighttime camps; the haunting cry of mountain lions shuddered the still air; bears rustled through the dense underbrush. The land seemed positively exotic. "You cannot imagine a sight so beautiful as this country," extolled traveler and writer Anne Royall in 1818, who through recording her thoughts in a narrative of her experiences during a stay in north Alabama managed to speak for untold thousands of contemporaries who did not or could not. "To compare it with the Elysian fields of the ancients, would give but a feeble idea of it."[1]

This wonderland came with its unsavory aspects, though. For one, it teemed with all manner of pest and vermin that could make life miserable and at times downright unbearable for man and beast for much of the year. Its climate could be at once welcoming and punishing. "The seasons are agreeable, the autumn and winter particularly," bragged one emigrants' guide in 1818, offering that "we know no place, where from September to April the weather is so "uniformly pleasant." Left unsaid in this description is something anyone who has ever lived in or visited Alabama knows: the area features brutally hot and long summers as well as stifling humidity. Trying to live in homes prior to air conditioning in these conditions, much less perform any sort of manual labor, could tax even the hardiest of souls. The area's brief winters could be surprisingly frigid. While this is still true today, Alabama's early years as part of the Mississippi Territory fell within what scientists term a "little ice age" characterized by overall cooler than normal temperatures and some of the most severe winters on record in the region. Temperatures in 1816, for example, remained below normal in part owing to a volcanic eruption in the Dutch East Indies that put so much ash into the atmosphere that regular climate patterns were temporarily interrupted throughout much of North America. The abnormally wintry air reputedly froze sea spray on the riggings of ships in Mobile Bay in the summer. Rainfall adequate for agriculture was a given in most years, but on occasion droughts struck that could devastate crops and ruin economies. Deadly tornadoes and hurricanes on occasion swept through the countryside, laying waste to huge swaths of territory and ferociously battering anything that stood in their way with a fearful suddenness. Such environmental conditions and the primitive state of medicine combined to help make illness and death an omnipresent threat to settlers. Life for them was much shorter, and much more unpredictable, than anything contemporary residents of Alabama can imagine.[2]

Yet thousands of American and European settlers piled into Alabama in the years after the Creek War with a heady optimism and contagious faith in the future rarely equaled at any other time in the state's long history. If the culture they gave birth to in hindsight seems a little unpolished at its genesis,

The John Looney House. Photograph by Mike Bunn.

it is owing at least in part to the fact that early settlers were preoccupied with the numerous chores involved in establishing their homes on the frontier. On arrival the great majority of early settlers immediately began the backbreaking work of preparing their houses and fields so that they might have shelter and food. Construction of a dwelling was the first priority. Log cabins—featuring hand-cut and notched logs pushed, pulled, and dragged into position—and barked slab roofs, popped up in wilderness clearings across the Alabama frontier. Inside their dimly lit interiors lay extremely few, utilitarian furnishings; a few iron pots, some glazed crockery, a few pieces of hand-hewn wooden furniture. As a family grew, these one-room cabins would often be enlarged by adding additional "pens" with a breezeway running between them to form the ubiquitous "dogtrot." Within a generation or two, many would be replaced by frame houses.[3]

Early Alabamians quite literally lived off the land, often making a great many of the things they needed in daily life from scratch with local materials, such as soap and medicine. Their most profound connection to the soil, though, lay in the fact that so many of them would feed their families and earn their living by farming. To prepare their fields, settlers commonly first burned away underbrush and girdled trees with an ax, creating "deadenings" in which their first crops would be planted—the "new ground." Within a few years, these small wilderness clearings would be widened and dead trees and other debris removed to yield a true open field. When they could, settlers hastened this process by taking advantage of natural clearings or fields previously cultivated in communal fashion by Native Americans. Alabama's landscape was altered faster and more profoundly in the decade after the Creek War than it had been for millennia as a consequence of all this agricultural activity. Innumerable farm fields previously concealed for centuries under forest cover suddenly lay exposed to the sun. It proved to be the beginning of a process of transforming the land that continues to this day.[4]

Herding became a primary agricultural pursuit among a large portion of early Alabamians. The expansive swaths of open lands made available to American settlers in Alabama were ideal for open range grazing by cattle and hogs, and many settlers tended herds as an avocation or just to provide themselves with steady supplies of meat, milk, and butter. Claims filed by citizens for damages during the Creek War of 1813–14, prior to the massive migration that defined Alabama's coming of age, reveal widespread herding activity already taking place among small farmers during the territorial days, as numerous claimants had the largest portion of their wealth tied up in cattle and hogs. Later, as new immigrants arrived in the territory to settle the land appropriated from the defeated Creeks, travelers observed herds of thousands of animals belonging to individual families on their journeys in the region. Virtually every farmer and plantation owner throughout the state maintained herds of some size.[5]

Even though cotton became the primary cash crop of most Alabamians, early settlers also grew enormous amounts of corn—the staff of life in early Alabama—and cultivated a variety of other vegetables. Peas, greens, and sweet potatoes, for example, found their way onto dinner tables and into regional markets and formed a core part of many people's diet. Early settlers subsisted on rather simple but abundant fare. Along with homegrown vegetables they dined on meat from both wild and domesticated animals, ranging from mutton to squirrel, but especially ham, beef, and venison. Decent water and milk, and not infrequently buttermilk, could usually be obtained in most places, with coffee something of a luxury. Whisky was ubiquitous. "Drinking was almost as common as eating," observed one of Alabama's first historians of the period, and every community of any size claimed at least one "grog shop."[6]

Even if fiercely independent, frontier farmers appreciated the help of neighbors—a term loosely applied to mean families living within a few miles of a homestead—in helping establish their homes. They relished opportunities to socialize in the process. Several families might gather to help one another with work such as clearing fields, raising cabins, shucking corn, and other tasks, turning the heavy labor required to make a living into a series of spirited contests over the course of several days. In the evening all would dine together and then perhaps dance to the strains of a fiddle or swap stories. Moments of merriment and small entertainments were savored. Friends and acquaintances took any opportunity that presented itself to break the monotony of secluded agricultural life by gathering to hunt, to gamble, to attend a horse race, a gander-pulling, a cockfight, or a camp meeting.[7]

Early Alabama communities, such as they were, developed in a rough-edged society almost as raw as the frontier on which they stood. Alabama settlers of course brought with them diverse folkways and worldviews shaped by their upbringing in other places. They adapted these over time to the circumstances they encountered in Alabama and drew on them in their eventual creation of a unique society. Early Alabama therefore featured not so much a monolithic culture with hard rules on behavior and etiquette as a blend of past experience and practicality shaped by an overarching pecuniary vision. Early settlers' efforts at community-building, after all, were more than anything else informed by the foundational, cross-class goal of securing economic success. For many that vision initially lay bound up more in notions of self-determination and rugged individualism than any conscious effort to create a new egalitarian society. Early Alabama encouraged and actually reveled in the rise of the often apocryphal "self-made man." This "cult of individualism," in the words of one historian, became instantly recognizable to observers of frontier culture and still informs our understanding of early Alabama society as it encouraged intense concentration on personal concerns often to the detriment of community-building.[8]

While in truth Alabama's settlers were no more or less uncivilized than those in any other frontier region of the country at the time, the colorful accounts by shocked new arrivals of life and culture in the territory and young state have left us with enduring, if exaggerated, descriptions of the uncouth manners and appearance of the region's people. Territorial judge Ephraim Kirby, for example, jotted down an almost humorous, if unflattering, description of his first impression of the inhabitants of the Tensaw region on his arrival in the early 1800s. For context he began his summation by observing that before the extension of federal law into the area it had long been the refuge of criminals and assorted outlaws who deemed it beyond the reach of legal authorities, or in Kirby's wording, those "who prefer voluntary exile to the punishments ordained by law." He went on to provide a sweeping indictment of the frontier culture he encountered by declaring that "the present inhabitants (with few exceptions) are illiterate, wild and savage, of depraved morals, unworthy of public confidence or private esteem; litigious, disunited, and knowing each other, universally distrustful of each other. . . . The administration of justice, imbecile and corrupt. The militia, without discipline or competent officers."[9]

Writing later from one of Alabama's largest cities on the cusp of statehood, lawyer Henry Hitchcock echoed Kirby's sentiments in a more urban environment. He disdained Mobile's citizenry as "rough and disagreeable," and expressed dismay that they had "little learning, less literature, and no refinement. There are few schools, and nothing of the regular system of learning . . . or government. . . . There are laws enough and good enough, but they are little regarded." Others, such as speculator William Ely, decried the slapdash architecture in Alabama's young cities and in exasperated fashion found fault with Alabamians' dress and manners:

> Of all the People I ever saw they are the most careless of their Cloaths. . . . To neatness & propriety in Dress both Sexes are, generally grossly inattentive: They all live in dirty, small, Sod & mud Cabins, or in those of a more mean construction & are generally almost destitute of all the Comforts & conveniences of Life. Bacon, corn bread, or greasy hot half baked biscuit, about as often without, as with vegetables, with Water, Buttermilk & sour milk, constitute, with Tea & Coffee, for those that buy them, their general Diet. . . . Much of the white Population of the State are extremely indolent, either too proud, or too lazy to work, or even think, they dissipate their time & money, & would their morals if they had any, without enjoyment, in lounging about Taverns, Stores, tipling houses, or in making & attending horse races, Cockfights, called here Chicken fights, shooting at a Mark, hunting or fighting. Notwithstanding such are their habits I think them a very avaricious People. Money is their God, & Cotton the Idol of their devotions.[10]

While Ely may have overplayed his neighbors' worship of money in his unsavory insinuation of their worldliness, the state was far removed from the church-centered Bible Belt society that conflated the temporal and spiritual realms in almost every aspect of the daily life that it became in later years. In actuality the young state in its terriorial years had relatively few churches; even in the largest communities such citizenry as attended worship services gathered primarily in private homes and public buildings such as courthouses until well into the 1820s. As with the development of political and economic infrastructure, however, the era witnessed the dawning of the rise of organized religion as a fundamental part of state society. The Baptist and Methodist denominations garnered the most popular appeal among Alabama's mostly yeoman citizenry that had the access and inclination to become involved with churches, as they eschewed a rigid formality and ecclesiastical orthodoxy in favor of more heartfelt spiritual conversions. By 1823 the Baptists had formed a state convention, including some 125 churches, virtually all of them less than a decade old and no few of them tended to by circuit-riding ministers preaching in each of several spots perhaps once a month. The Methodists, however, could claim even more responsibility for laying the foundation for the rise of evangelical Protestantism to become a guiding force in Alabama's culture. In their famed camp meetings, sometimes as much spectacle and wilderness party as pious gathering, they brought religion to the masses and made their brand of Christianity open to all. A Huntsville newspaper carried one of the best descriptions of the nature and spirit of a camp meeting to appear in print in early Alabama in 1823:

> A favorable spot in the woods was selected as the place of worship, and a crude pulpit and altar was erected. Benches were arranged around this, and tents for the accommodation of tables and guests were pitched about the ground. Two sermons were usually preached in the morning, and then a short recess was allowed for dinner. At this time, the worshippers would repair to the tents where abundant supplies of food were laid out for the benefit of all. People from the surrounding country came on horseback, in carriages, or afoot, as circumstances permitted, bringing their picnic lunches with them. The occasion was one of social as well as religious enjoyment, and crowds of thousands were sometimes assembled to hear favorite exhorters. After dinner, the services were resumed, and they were always concluded by an invitation to repentant sinners to come up to the altar. Large numbers usually went forward, and as the minister prayed for them, the congregation went into a religious ecstasy of praying, moaning, and shouting. But it must not be inferred that these were disorderly gatherings. There was a spirit of sociability and festivity on the part of the people and of gravity on the part of the leaders which gave them a dignity of their own.[11]

Other religious groups, including the Presbyterian and Catholic Churches, were active in early Alabama as well, though not enjoying the same broad base of appeal as the Baptists and the Methodists. Catholicism laid claim to being the first version of Christianity practiced in the state, having been introduced

Depiction of a frontier camp meeting. Courtesy of the Library of Congress.

by the French when they founded Mobile, and of course practiced even earlier by the Spanish during their short-lived explorations of portions of the future state in the sixteenth and seventeenth centuries. The Catholic Church languished in Alabama during its early statehood years despite its long history; however, it was a distinct minority in an overwhelmingly Protestant state. When the Vicariate Apostolic of Alabama and Florida was established in the 1820s, Mobile hosted the lone documented Catholic church in the state.[12]

Even though early Alabama featured a mostly rural population, strategically located cities popped up throughout the state in the late 1810s and into the early 1820s. Almost as many trading centers were planned as towns organically developed during the era. These urban centers were a far cry from what many contemporary readers might imagine as a city. Dirty, earthy places featuring closely situated and low-slung wooden buildings arranged somewhat haphazardly, they had dirt streets that became dusty in dry weather and muddy when wet. As early Alabama towns could often be home to as many animals as people, through them traveled an incongruent stream of carriages, wagons, businessmen, farmers, slaves, and a variety of dogs, cats, chickens, horses, mules, pigs, and even the occasional cow. The pungent odors such an assemblage of men and beasts might generate in a hot and humid environment with no

Site of the "Big Spring" in downtown Huntsville, around which the community developed in the first decades of the nineteenth century. Photograph by Mike Bunn.

running water, no sewers, and no air conditioning, combined with the acrid scent of smoke from numerous kitchens and hearths, hung heavy in the air at all times.[13]

While many cities came and went within a few years, others took root and survive to this day. In the Tennessee Valley, the city of Huntsville had been in existence less than a decade at the time of statehood but already laid claim to a level of sophistication reserved for communities much older. Investors led by surveyor and Creek War hero John Coffee developed nearby Florence, predicted to be the "entrepôt of the Tennessee," as Alabama transitioned from territory to state. Along the Black Warrior at the same time a humble village that would eventually become home to the state capital and the state university, Tuscaloosa, had begun to take shape. Meanwhile, on the banks of the Alabama River three towns near the site of venerable Indian villages were beginning to move toward consolidation as the city of Montgomery. Selma and the future capital of Cahawba were laid out during the territorial years on promising spots previously occupied by lone settlers. Near the geographic center of the state a determined woman named Sarah F. Chotard planned what she envisioned as a future trading center and potential state capital along the Cahaba River, the appropriately named city of "Centreville." Chotard had arrived in

Alabama in 1820 armed with a grant for 1,500 acres of her choosing for the scheme and tried without success to persuade no less a figure than Andrew Jackson—whom she may or may not have known—to endorse the effort. She died in 1824 with her dreams unrealized, but the city she founded survives.[14]

In the extreme southern portion of the territory, on opposite sides of the Mobile-Tensaw Delta, stood two cities that epitomized early Alabama's urban scene. Mobile, ancient by the standards of the time, having been founded in 1702 by the French and moved to its current site in 1711, was transitioning from backwater military outpost to maritime trading emporium. Already the seasonal cotton shipping activity along its waterfront and financing of its trade from downtown offices were combining to transform the otherwise sleepy town into a vital link in the international cotton trade. Mobile also claimed Alabama's only sizable population of free blacks, consisting of the community of creoles who traced their ancestry back to the original Europeans and African occupants of the humid Gulf Coast colonial outposts. On the opposite side of the labyrinth of rivers emptying into Mobile Bay stood Blakeley, a city whose first lots had gone up for sale in 1814. Its namesake founder, Josiah Blakeley, envisioned the community as a cross-bay competitor to Mobile owing to its deep-water port along the Tensaw River. Blakeley briefly blossomed into one of Alabama's fastest-growing cities and primary ports before a host of setbacks, especially the repeated outbreak of the dreaded viral disease yellow fever, doomed it to become a ghost town.[15]

The establishment of a community newspaper by enterprising private printers ranked perhaps foremost among the many events that marked a city's coming of age during the era, in the eyes of many. Early Alabama's towns developed during an age in which the primary public source of news for Americans throughout the country consisted of daily and weekly broadsheets, and almost any city large enough to support a modest circulation had, or attempted to sustain, at least one paper. Newspapers had been established within what became Alabama as early as 1811, but by 1819, on the heels of the wave of immigration to the new state, at least ten had been established in its emerging principal cities. Carrying such colorful names as the *Sun*, the *Courier*, the *Halcyon*, and the *Intelligencer*, these periodicals, often short-lived and frequently changing editors and locations, offered reprints of articles from other newspapers, a variety of editorials, occasional poetry and short stories, and an abundance of advertisements that serve as one of the most telling gauges of economic activity in the communities they served. Notices for an incredible variety of early Alabama businesses could be found within their pages: dry

Modern downtown Mobile, the heart of Alabama's oldest city, today rises from the riverfront plain the French originally settled over three hundred years ago. Photograph by Mike Bunn.

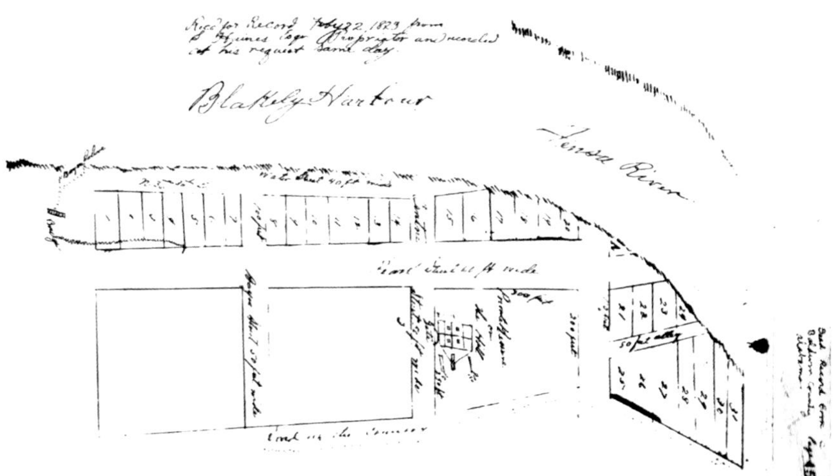

Map of a portion of Blakeley. Courtesy of the Alabama Department of Archives and History.

goods and hardware stores, grocers, hotels, clothiers, booksellers, blacksmiths, private academies, stagecoach and steamboat lines, and so on. As Alabama's cities grew in size and sophistication in the early 1820s, increasingly within the pages of newspapers in the larger communities appeared notices of things that revealed another type of coming of age—show times at theaters (traveling and local), schedules for horse races, and the services of artisans such as silversmiths and portrait painters.[16]

The temporary nature of the construction of many buildings in Alabama's early urban centers, the ravages of the elements, and patterns of use all combined to diminish their architectural heritage over time and complicate our contemporary efforts to envision them as they once were. Nothing could alter a cityscape faster or with more devastating finality as fire, however. Fire struck terror in the hearts of early Alabama's city dwellers in a palpable fashion foreign to those of us living today. Manpower or equipment would seldom be equal to the task of combating a raging inferno once started even if equipment could be assembled, since piped water was unavailable. Since cities of the era commonly featured clusters of closely situated wooden structures, they were virtual tinderboxes that, once ignited, might blaze until the fires died out from lack of fuel. Conflagrations engulfed whole blocks of period communities with startling regularity in the early nineteenth century. In Mobile, for example, large fires swept through the city in 1820, 1822, and 1827, destroying virtually all of what was left of its territorial-period architecture and redefining its appearance. In others brick and mortar construction began to replace the deteriorating original wooden structures within a decade, and as cities grew, new and larger buildings on wide, planned streets erased much of the original character of these early settlements.[17]

Prior to the Great Migration, which brought so many settlers to Alabama, the region had in large part been a wilderness region inhabited primarily by groups of Native Americans, far removed from the American mainstream. In less than a decade its American population had skyrocketed and, in the process of the new settlers' efforts to harness its abundant resources and create new trading centers, given rise to the ruggedly independent society from which the state of Alabama would emerge. As a consequence, in incredibly short order, Alabama began its move from backwoods frontier to assume a key position in the developing American South.

Five

THE LAND CALLED ALABAMA

From Territory to State

Alabama finally came into its own as an independent territory in 1817. Over the course of the next two tumultuous years, it established the broad outlines of its government and rapidly moved toward statehood even as serious regional rivalries emerged that threatened consensus on a variety of issues.

By 1817 the Mississippi Territory had been in existence for nineteen years, by far the longest territorial period by any state experienced to date. Its recent growth seemed to assure imminent statehood, but the manner in which it would enter the union remained a point of great contention. Would the territory become one state or two? Where would the border be drawn if it were divided? Where would its center(s) of government be located in either scenario? Deciding these paramount political questions would not only determine the course of Alabama's path toward statehood but also expose the growing sectional rivalries that would influence its early development.

The long-standing antipathy between the Mississippi Territory's eastern and western sections became the first to come to the fore. The area of American settlement along the rivers immediately north of Mobile had felt neglected and overshadowed by the territory's Mississippi River settlements virtually from its

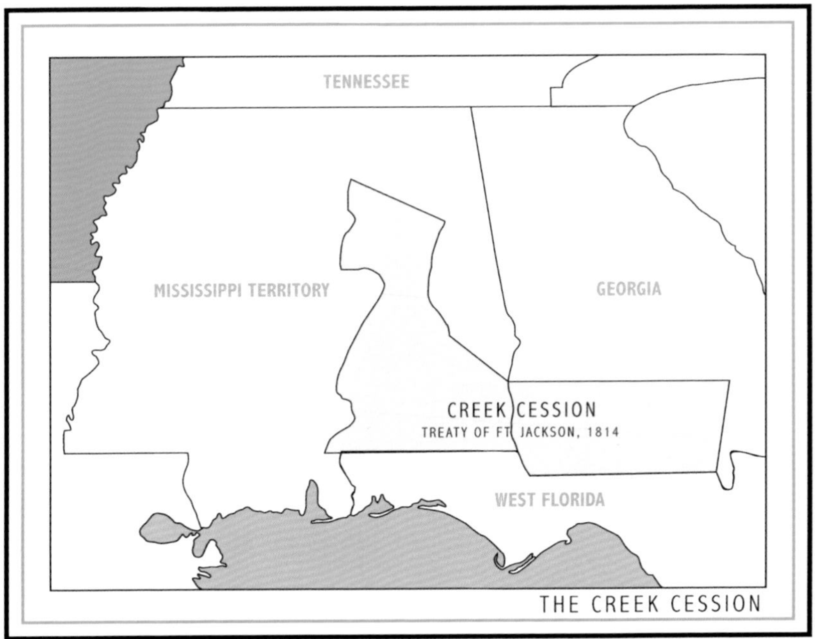

Map showing the territory ceded by the Creeks as a result of the Treaty of Fort Jackson, from Bunn and Williams *Battle for the Southern Frontier: The Creek War and the War of 1812*.

founding. Early on, citizens in these settlements advocated for division of the territory, at one point even urging the creation of an independent "Mobile Territory." Leaders in the Natchez area, on the other hand, were keenly aware of the economic and political dominance of their region in the territory's affairs and desired to see it enter the union as a single state and Natchez remain its capital. This internal squabbling stymied efforts by congressional delegates George Poindexter and William Lattimore to move the territory toward statehood prior to the War of 1812. The territory's unwieldy size worked against their efforts, as well, since, in the words of a Senate committee report drafted after a review of one proposal for statehood, it stood "disproportionate to the size of any of the largest states which now compose our confederation." Further complicating matters was the fact that, owing to the terms of the agreement in which Georgia relinquished previous claims to the land, statehood for the Mississippi Territory required that state's approval.[1]

The situation only became more complicated at the end of the Creek War. Owing to the fact that millions of acres of some of the richest cotton lands in the nation had been ceded to the United States by the defeated Creeks in the territory's eastern section, a switching of the long-standing positions on statehood suddenly occurred. Eastern section residents, now seeing the likelihood of dynamic growth in the near future, anticipated ascendancy in regional affairs. In addition, the rapidly growing city of Huntsville and nearby Tennessee Valley settlements—neither of which had existed when debate over division began but by 1815 ranked among its largest population centers—further augured potential eastern section dominance. As a consequence, easterners began pushing for the Mississippi Territory to be admitted to the union as a single state, while westerners, observing how their rival section had begun to outstrip them in population and economic activity, began to contemplate division.[2]

Finding it impossible to follow the contradictory and shifting opinions of those he represented, delegate Lattimore decided to pursue division as the most practical approach. He was working closely with Senator Charles Tait of Georgia to move toward statehood in the fall of 1816 when disgruntled locals called a special meeting at the home of prominent minister and government official, John Ford, along the Pearl River to discuss how they might pursue statehood on their terms, however. Dominated by easterners, this "Pearl River Convention" attempted to counter Lattimore by drafting a memorial to Congress asking for immediate statehood with current borders intact and appointing Judge Harry Toulmin as their delegate in Washington. In the end Lattimore and Tait successfully pushed through their plan for division despite Toulmin's interference. The boundary as authorized by Congress began at the Gulf of Mexico about ten miles east of Pascagoula, ran north to the northwest corner of the boundary of Washington County, then northeastward to the point where Bear Creek emptied into the Tennessee River, then along that river to the Tennessee state line. On March 1, 1817, Congress approved the enabling act that authorized the western section of the territory to prepare for admission to the union as the state of Mississippi and on March 3 approved an act creating the Alabama Territory from the eastern section. The latter act stipulated that the territorial government it authorized in Alabama would become effective as soon as Mississippi formed a constitution and state government. While neither section thought the border exactly suited their wishes, especially since it divided the settlements of the Tombigbee River basin and separated Mobile and closely affiliated Pascagoula, they realized further fighting would only delay statehood for both. Mississippi drafted its constitution and entered the union on December 10, 1817. Alabama assumed territorial status simultaneously and put plans in motion for the convening of its own legislature in January 1818.[3]

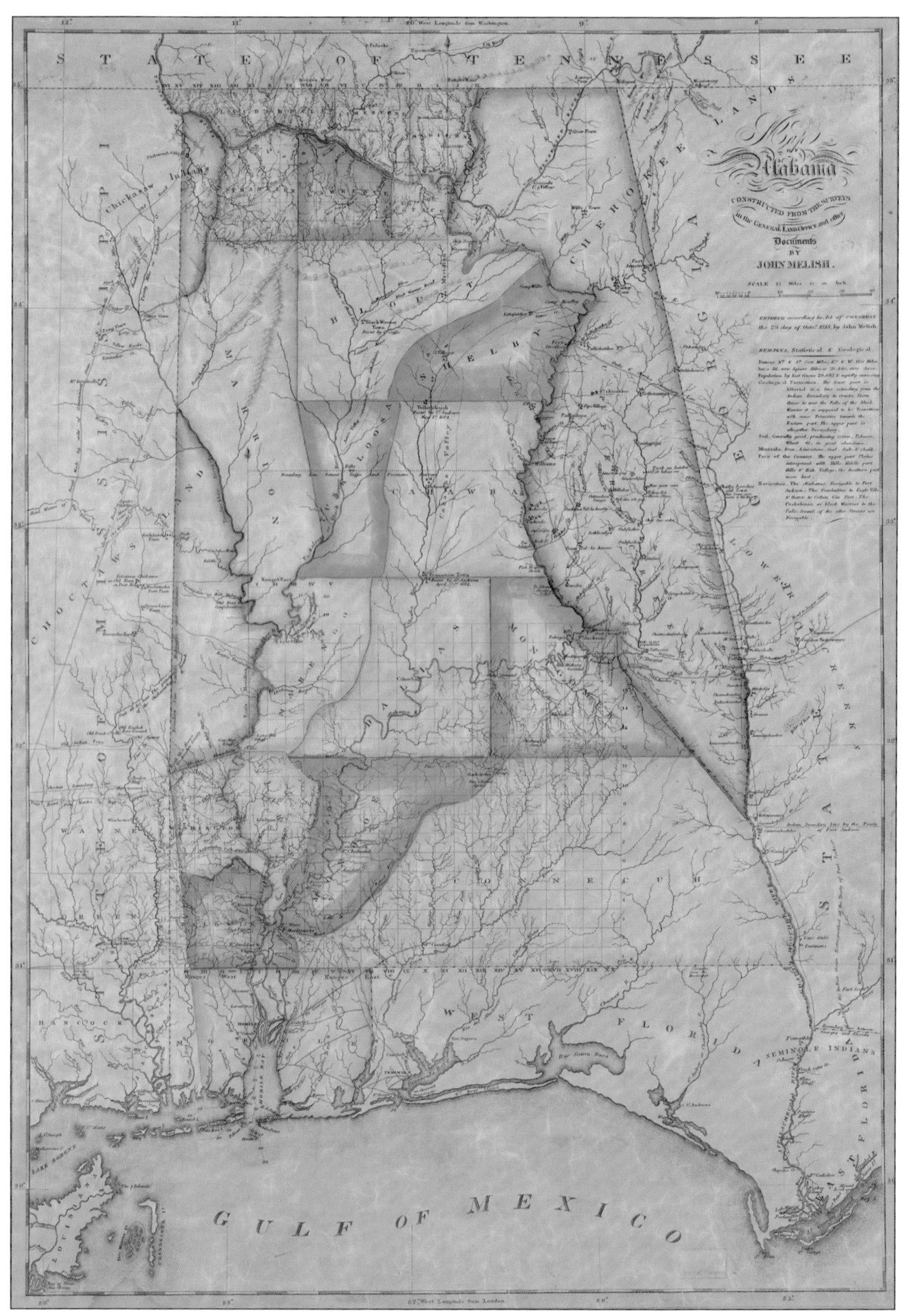

Map of Alabama Territory, 1818, by John Melish. Courtesy of the Library of Congress.

Governor William Wyatt Bibb. Courtesy of the Alabama Department of Archives and History.

President James Monroe appointed William Wyatt Bibb, a trained doctor, veteran politician, and recent but well-connected arrival in Alabama, as governor of the new Alabama Territory. Along with his brother, Thomas, who had preceded him in moving to Alabama, and other influential friends who would soon follow, Bibb's administration would inaugurate a period of remarkable influence by a small group of wealthy Georgians from that state's Broad River region that historians today recognize as Alabama's first serious political party. Alabama came of age in what historians often term the Era of Good Feelings, an interlude in American political history characterized by general rising prosperity, optimism, and a preoccupation with expansion rather than the partisan squabbles that characterized what came immediately before and after. The territory and early state nevertheless contained serious political factions, with the Broad River group being by far the most influential. Through their wealth and connections in the nation's capital, the group in many ways reigned over political life in the territory as if it were a virtual fiefdom. They managed to appoint themselves or their friends to almost every significant office in the territorial and early state governments. Sometimes referred to by their detractors at the time as the "Royal Party," in addition to the Bibb brothers this powerful cadre of Alabama founders included Charles Tait, John W. Walker, and wealthy planter LeRoy Pope. These men were allied with influential friends in Washington, such as US secretary of the Treasury William H. Crawford. Tait would eventually guide the bill for Alabama's statehood through Congress and become the first federal district judge in the new state; Pope, who had already helped establish the town of Huntsville, would preside over Madison County's first county court and serve as a commissioner of the Planters and Merchants Bank; John W. Walker would serve in the territorial legislature, preside over the state's constitutional convention, and serve as one of Alabama's first US senators.[4]

The act creating the Alabama Territory called for elected officials representing the area in the Mississippi Territory's General Assembly to serve the remainder of their terms as members of Alabama's first governing body. It also designated Saint Stephens as their meeting place. On January 19, 1818, fourteen legislators gathered there at the Douglas Hotel for the Alabama Territory's inaugural legislative session. Thirteen of those present held membership in the legislature's lower house; only one councilor from the body's upper house, James Titus, attended. In this and a second session held in November, the Alabama Territory General Assembly established the inner workings of government and organized basic services for its citizenry. The legislature passed a flurry of laws in a matter of weeks, including the chartering of Alabama's first school (Saint Stephens Academy) and bank (Tombeckbe), and the naming of Creek Indian agent John Crowell to represent Alabama as its delegate in the nation's capital. The General Assembly also organized over a dozen new counties in the land it administered in the course of its proceedings.[5]

None of the dozens of statutes the General Assembly considered in those first two sessions involved quite as much energy or passion as the debate over the selection of a future state capital. Saint Stephens, located in the extreme southwest of the territory, clearly would be replaced as seat of government once statehood occurred. But since the designation of a new capital city would mean a great deal of prestige, influence, and coveted economic activity in whichever region it was located, the battle for that title starkly exposed the new mounting rivalry between north (meaning the Tennessee Valley) and south Alabama (meaning the virtual remainder). While almost every corner of Alabama featured rapid growth, the pace of development in north Alabama proved truly exceptional. In the fall of 1818 Madison County alone laid claim to approximately a sixth of the entire territory's population and accounted for about a quarter of all taxes paid into its treasury. Neighboring Tennessee Valley counties such as Lauderdale, Lawrence, Limestone, and Cotaco (future Morgan) also had sizeable and swiftly growing populations that in sheer numbers and pace of development as a group outstripped almost everything to their south. It soon became obvious that this imbalance threatened to play havoc in Alabama's political affairs.[6]

Fully aware of Alabama's population dynamics, the commission formed to find a centrally located site for a state capital recommended Tuscaloosa as a compromise between north and south Alabama. During the interim between meetings of the legislature in the summer of 1818, however, Governor Bibb busily worked to establish a capital farther south at the junction of the Cahaba and Alabama Rivers, where he envisioned a great city. Tapping connections in Washington, he obtained federal grants of land for the scheme and in his address delivered to the legislature at the opening of its inaugural session revealed his plan for Alabama's "scite [*sic*] of Government." In sealing the deal, south Alabama legislators made several concessions to their counterparts in north Alabama, who sought to leverage their larger population to fullest advantage in return for allowing the future state's seat of government to be located along the Cahaba. They directed that Huntsville would serve temporarily as state capital until facilities in the planned city of Cahawba could actually be built—something far from certain in the eyes of many—and only if the still-imaginary town remained the capital in 1825 could it be declared permanent. In a related and perhaps even more important matter, north Alabama legislators also won passage of their plan for apportionment in the constitutional convention that would be called once Congress approved Alabama's statehood. Representation in that body would be determined solely on the basis of each county's white population—a decided advantage to the overall more populous north Alabama counties, which contained a smaller percentage of slaves per capita than many of the south Alabama counties—with no limits placed on the number of representatives an individual county might have.[7]

Despite the confidence and speed with which the territory's political leaders moved it toward statehood, reminders of how recently even its most populous areas lay in native hands could be seen everywhere. The heart of the territory then available for settlement still lay flanked, east and west, by the remnants of a Native American domain claimed by four powerful tribes—the

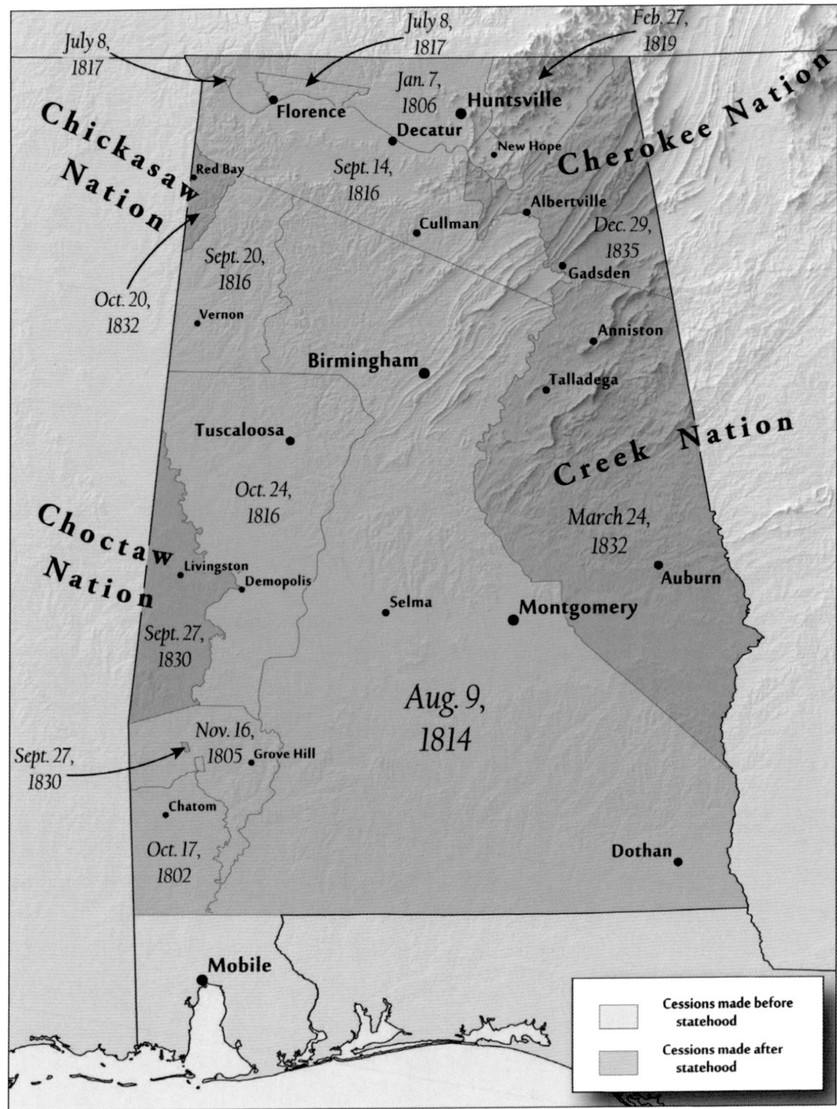

Land ceded in Alabama by Indian tribes, 1806–35. Courtesy of the University of Alabama Cartographic Research Library.

Creek, Choctaw, Chickasaw, and Cherokee—which remained foreign nations though technically within the territory's boundaries. Portions of these ancestral lands would remain in native possession for another generation, but their ultimate surrender to the inexorably expanding United States seemed foreordained to its new arrivals. The suddenness of this transition of ownership proved remarkable. Barely over a decade prior to the first meeting of the Alabama Territory's legislature, only two small tracts of land, located in its extreme north and southwest, legally had been opened to American settlement. The lion's share had been ceded between 1814 and 1816. Thus, in the span of a short three years the population dynamic of the entire region had been reversed and the Indians found themselves clinging to the fringes of the borders of new territory. Writer Anne Royall's account of the breakneck speed with which this exchange played out in Alabama's Tennessee River Valley area reads as a profound Alabama allegory: "This land was abandoned last fall by the Indians. The fires were still smoking, when the white people took possession."[8]

Alabama's Native Americans had of course not watched passively as all this played out. Skilled in international diplomacy through negotiation with multiple colonial powers vying for influence in their homeland for over a century, they had managed to maintain their autonomy until the Revolutionary War replaced several relatively weak rivals with a single American juggernaut. Unable to play one rival off another any longer and seeing their territories incrementally reduced, they found themselves at a severe disadvantage economically, politically, and militarily. The devastating defeat of the Creeks in 1814 graphically illustrated their plight. Generations of involvement in global trading networks had transformed Alabama's native groups, however, and they were anything but provincial primitives. Native Americans in the Alabama Territory were if anything more urban than their American neighbors, especially the Creeks, whose entire society formed around the dozens of towns in which they lived. Some of these were quite large by the standards of the day, containing well over one thousand residents at a time in which only the largest American settlements in the region contained about the same number. They farmed the same crops as their American neighbors, often with slave labor; sometimes operated businesses such as inns and ferries; and not infrequently had intermarried with white families to the point that some of their most influential leaders of the era carried names such as McGillivray, McIntosh, Weatherford, Perryman, and Colbert. The Colberts, brothers and Chickasaw chiefs George and Levi, personified this new type of Native American leader emerging as Alabama moved toward statehood. Astride two worlds, they would wield influence in both. The Colberts helped negotiate treaties between the Chickasaws and Americans, operated assorted business enterprises catering to an American clientele, and employed slave labor on their expansive plantations. Of more enduring fame, perhaps, were the accomplishments of a Cherokee leader named Sequoyah who lived in northeast Alabama during the years it transitioned from territory to statehood. Through years of study and experimentation, he perfected a syllabary for the Cherokee language that would allow the spoken language to be recorded in writing.[9]

Native Americans nevertheless became relegated to second-class status in early Alabama. Being encouraged to abandon their ancestral ways but never fully welcomed into American society, they occupied a tenuous middle ground in which they were at best tolerated and at worst feared and despised by their neighbors. Many, if not most, early American settlers regarded Native Americans as mere "savages" and never could bring themselves to accept that Native Americans had the same rights to the land as they had or could ever be suited to citizenship. Still, early Alabama's history is replete with examples of bonds of friendship and affection between individual settlers and Indians. Even the man who helped oversee removal of the Choctaws from Alabama, agent and politician George Strother Gaines, would in his later years admit that during his service in Alabama's territorial period he saw in Choctaw culture much that "caused both surprise and admiration," grudgingly allowing in hindsight that "they were not such savages as I had imagined." Other, less biased, observers found in them a praiseworthy dignity few residents of the time could have countenanced in public discourse. In the diary he kept during his travel within the Creek Nation in 1824, Swiss citizen Lukas Vischer, for example, recorded his respect for their friendliness, good tastes, practicality, and craftsmanship, offering that "these Indians are in general handsome people, well built and of splendid bearing, and their clothing is handsome and the decorations on the same exceedingly tasteful." Vischer also witnessed in the Creeks an innate talent for diplomacy and tact in even the most delicate of matters. When requesting information on Indian religion, he noted that his guide, Chilly McIntosh, attempted to explain the fundamental differences in theological worldview between the Creeks and the mostly Protestant Christian Americans in a way that did not assert one of the two correct and the other in error. Instead, he merely offered that the Creeks did "believe in God, and in heaven and hell . . . they sing but do not pray, because God has not taught them how they ought to speak with him."[10]

Yet for all this evidence of accommodation and coexistence, even if reluctantly, startling reminders that the Alabama Territory lay within a still-contested frontier region manifested themselves from time to time. In the winter of 1817/18 the smoldering embers of the fiery spirit of resistance of the Red Stick Creeks rekindled among a remnant of the defeated nation and their Seminole cousins in Florida. What began as localized disputes over trespassing and cattle theft along the Georgia-Florida border abruptly flared up into a regional

Upper Creek Chief Opothle Yoholo, from a lithograph by Thomas L. McKenney and James Hall, after a portrait by Charles Bird King. Courtesy of the Library of Congress.

confrontation that would become known as the First Seminole War. Isolated acts of violence flashed throughout the southern half of the territory and threatened to pull Alabama into the conflict, none more provocative than the massacre of the Stroud and Ogly families in Monroe County on March 13, 1818, by a group of renegades led by a Creek man known as Savannah Jack. In the grisly carnage of a surprise attack, members of both families, including several children, were cruelly butchered. Forts built for the protection of settlers began to pop up that spring, bearing such names as Dale, Gay, Bibb, and Butler, and older posts, including Fort Mitchell and Fort Crawford, assumed a new strategic importance. In the first true crisis of his administration, Governor Bibb personally visited some of the stockades, sought the assistance of allied Creeks and the federal government, and ordered militia in pursuit of the hostile raiders. The emergency proved to be short-lived in Alabama, however, as the focus of attention soon turned exclusively to Florida once Andrew Jackson invaded the Spanish province to put down the Seminole threat. Their attention refocused, territorial leaders quickly resumed their headlong pursuit of statehood.[11]

Barely a year after being established, that goal appeared imminent. Early in 1819 the matter came up for discussion in Congress, spurred on by powerful friends such as Senator Charles Tait and the informed lobbying of local leaders such as John W. Walker. In a particularly resonant petition sent during the territory's final legislative session, for example, Walker insisted that Alabama's citizens "cannot conceive, how it could promote the interest of the national government, longer, to withhold from the people of Alabama the right they solicit." He reminded Congress of the "unparalleled tide of emigration" washing over the region and that, with a population of nearly seventy thousand (white) people, the Alabama Territory easily surpassed the population of Mississippi and compared favorably to other recently admitted states. With Tait's guidance, the statehood bill at last cleared Congress, and on March 2, 1819, President James Monroe signed the act that enabled the formation of a government for the state of Alabama. Elections were to be held in May to choose delegates to a constitutional convention scheduled for July. As if to underscore Alabama's impending arrival on the national scene, on June 1 President Monroe paid a surprise visit to Huntsville while on a whirlwind tour of the southern states. At a hastily arranged banquet in his honor, local leading lights paid their respects to the nation's leader in series of toasts. Monroe responded with one of his own for the Alabama Territory: "May her speedy admission into the Union advance her happiness, and augment the national strength and prosperity."[12]

Alabama's constitutional convention opened in a vacant cabinet shop in Huntsville on July 5, 1819. Forty-four delegates representing the territory's twenty-two counties—eight of them from host Madison County—attended. It ranked as a distinguished group by frontier standards; from the convention would come several of the future state's governors, judges of its Supreme Court, senators, and even a vice president of the United States (William Rufus de Vane King). John W. Walker served as the convention's president, but, according to at least one witness, "informally and with little decorum." Professionally led or not, the convention's members took their business seriously and immediately set to work by creating a subcommittee of fifteen to draft the constitution and busied themselves with the body's housekeeping and numerous other smaller associated matters that demanded attention. Working six days a week throughout July, they soon had a completed document that the convention approved and signed on August 2, 1819.[13]

Reconstruction of the cabinet shop in Huntsville where the constitutional convention met in 1819. Photograph by Mike Bunn.

The constitution proved a relatively liberal governing instrument for the time, broadly reflecting the interests of the new state's significant yeomen farmer population and exhibiting a special understanding of Alabama's frontier nature. It called for universal adult white male suffrage with no property, taxpayer status, or militia service qualifications. Requirements for holding office were likewise minimal, the framers having eschewed traditional property qualifications. Acknowledging a fact of life in a state undergoing a dramatic increase in population, the constitution stipulated short periods of residency for candidates for office. The constitution called for the popular election of judges rather than their appointment, included a bill of rights, established a state-owned bank, and detailed specific measures for the advancement of education such as dedicating a section of land in every township for that purpose and establishing a state university. Although Alabama's governing document expressly sanctioned the institution of human slavery, it paid at least lip service to encouraging humane treatment of bondsmen by owners, guaranteeing slaves some limited fundamental rights, and setting specific criteria for emancipation. Per their instructions, the framers sent their constitution directly to Congress, not to the people of Alabama, for approval. The end of Alabama's protracted territorial experience, now approaching its twenty-first anniversary, finally appeared in sight.[14]

Six

ALABAMA

From Old Southwest to Old South

Following nearly two decades as part of the Mississippi Territory and two years as an independent territory, Alabama at last became a state in 1819. In its first few years of statehood, it managed to find a degree of stability that would place it on a trajectory to become a dynamic and influential part of the American Union only by surviving political disruption, an economic crisis, and a contentious debate over the permanent location of its seat of government.

Virtually as soon as the gavel closing the proceedings of Alabama's constitutional convention fell, campaigning for seats in the first session of the General Assembly of the State of Alabama, called for October, began. In late September 1819, twenty-two senators and fifty representatives won election to the state's new legislature. Although the race for the state's chief executive ended up being tighter than might have been expected, territorial governor William Wyatt Bibb secured the honor of also heading Alabama's first state government.[1]

Alabama's state legislature opened its first session on October 25, 1819, in Huntsville. Governor Bibb attempted to impress on the legislators the solemnity of the occasion in a written address read to the body at its commencement, observing the gathering would "form a memorable epoch in our history," though they likely needed no reminders of the importance of the

President James Monroe. Courtesy of the Library of Congress.

work before them. They indeed took it seriously, over the course of the next seven weeks passing some seventy-seven acts designed to bring the constitution into practical effect. Legislative acts passed ranged from routine matters such as setting the salaries of state officials to a rather aspirational appropriation for an engineering survey to determine the best way to connect—ostensibly via canal—the Tennessee and Mobile River systems. While the dream of linking the state's two major river systems would not be completed for over a century and a half despite significant planning in the state's early years, other goals were accomplished immediately. The legislature established a court system, outlined rules and regulations for the establishment of a state militia, and, in a glaring reflection of the type of society in which Alabama emerged, codified procedures for the establishment of a means to patrol slaves. It also organized a taxation structure that relied in large part on assessments on various forms of property to provide the revenue necessary for the government's operation. Mindful as ever to balance political spoils among north and south Alabama, legislators chose John W. Walker of Huntsville and William Rufus de Vane King of Selma as the state's first United States senators.[2]

As the General Assembly prepared to bring its proceedings to a close in mid-December, the congressional resolution admitting Alabama into the union finally came to President Monroe's desk in Washington. He signed it on December 14, 1819, and Alabama officially became the twenty-second state of the United States of America. Meanwhile, the legislature, having its business accomplished, authorized the body's doorkeeper to sell at auction the very furniture it had used during its deliberations; the state would get a literal as well as figurative fresh start the next year in the new capital being carved from the wilderness in the central section of the state.[3]

What should have been an unsullied moment of exultant triumph, however, was somewhat muted by economic uncertainty. The year 1819 in many ways stands as among the least auspicious of Alabama's tumultuous territorial experience. Shortly after the turn of the new year in 1819, a land heretofore showcasing steady economic growth, generous and easy credit, wide-ranging speculation, and general optimism among a swelling population suddenly plunged into a severe economic downturn. Known to historians as the Panic of 1819, this first major depression in US history struck Alabama particularly hard and carried with it far-ranging repercussions that would resonate well into its first decade of statehood. The root causes of the depression are tangled and complex, but at its heart lay a combination of overextension of credit in the heady years after the War of 1812, a rash of unregulated banking and questionable financial management of the Second Bank of the United States, lowered demand for cotton in Europe as overseas mills began to tap into markets in India, and declining prices for manufactured goods. Alabama essentially became the front lines of the disaster in the South. Cotton and land sales its fledgling banks financed were the very lifeblood of its economic engine; when the markets for both ground to a halt so did the new state's economy.[4]

In early 1819 the first tremors of the impending calamity hit when cotton prices began to falter. By summer they had plummeted to as low as twelve cents per pound after an extended period in which they averaged over twice that and at times had reached over thirty cents per pound. The cascading series of disasters that resulted brought widespread economic ruin over much of Alabama for an extended period as shaken financial institutions suspended issuance of loans and countless debtors defaulted on existing mortgages for the soil they tilled. The financial collapse unraveled the very fabric of frontier communities across the territory, as the informal and unregulated methods of extending credit and repaying debt—often sealed with little more than handshakes and letters of recommendation obligating friends and family as security on loans—collapsed on itself like so many dominoes and swamped communities in wholesale fashion. By some estimates as much as half the land debt in the nation lay in Alabama at the onset of the depression, and in its depths, debtors ended up relinquishing enormous swaths of acreage. In the Huntsville area alone, some four hundred thousand acres were reclaimed by the federal government within a span of just three years. Reactions to the economic reverses ranged from fleeing the scene to suicide.[5]

A slow but steady economic recovery, coupled with the passage of the federal Land Relief Act of 1821, allowing debtors to renegotiate the terms of their loans for a portion of their lands, eventually brought the state through the worst of the crisis. Still, the ramifications of the depression were profound and extended far beyond the purely economic realm in Alabama. In some ways it redefined the landscape of its political terrain, since in finding a scapegoat for the calamity Alabamians believed they discovered their former heroes from Georgia might just have been a self-serving cabal. The roots of the demise of the "Royal Party," like the crisis itself, are tangled and deep, but they can be traced to the remarkable degree with which the small group of influential Georgians and their affiliates had managed to consolidate power. Since they held leadership positions in Alabama's legislature and in its financial institutions, when the financial storm struck they came under brutal scrutiny. There had been rumblings of discontent with the supposed haughtiness of some of them prior to the depression; as early as 1810 some people in north Alabama were outraged when LeRoy Pope managed to bring about a change in the name of the community that sprang up around John Hunt's home from Huntsville to the rather patrician-sounding Twickenham (in honor of the home of the British poet Alexander Pope, whom Pope held in high esteem but bore no relation). But in the hectic growth in the wake of the Alabama Territory's formation, few had seemed to give the matter of the Georgian's growing influence more than passing notice. Nor had any uproar taken place back in 1818 when, in what hindsight revealed to be an epic miscalculation wrought of a combination of unbridled optimism and uncloaked greed, Royal Party affiliates had pushed through legislation abolishing all limitations on the amount of interest that could be charged on loans.[6]

That some of them were associated with the embattled Planters and Merchants Bank would come to hang, albatross-like, around their collective necks as the depression dismantled homesteads the next year. Under the heat of the spotlight resentful antagonists such as Huntsville editor William Long steadily applied, even former steadfast allies would seek to distance themselves from the Georgians, and they began to lose the hold on the reins of power they had so long held. The sudden death of Governor William W. Bibb, a pivotal leader of the Georgian affiliates, only hastened the changing of the guard. Already weakened from tuberculosis, he suffered a bad fall while riding a horse on his plantation in Autauga County early in 1820 and lay bedridden for weeks before succumbing at length to internal injuries in July at the age of just thirty-nine. The new state constitution called for the president of the senate to assume the position of governor should that official become unable to serve, a position ironically enough held at the time by Bibb's brother, Thomas. Thomas Bibb served the remainder of his brother's term as governor and headed the first legislative session convened in the fall at Cahawba. During that session, legislators determined to honor the man who had guided Alabama through its years as an independent territory, shepherded it through the process of statehood, and planned its capital, by renaming Cahawba County as Bibb County.[7]

The story of the rise of the capital city of Cahawba, which had been Bibb's dream, is an example in microcosm of Alabama's development during the early statehood era. The town lay at the confluence of the Alabama and its namesake Cahaba Rivers, a location that people had recognized as strategically important for centuries before Governor Bibb extolled its virtues. Even as surveyors marked out its lots, the remnants of a large fortified Mississippian-era town reminded newcomers that Native Americans had inhabited the place prior to their arrival. More recently, the townsite had been the home of a lone squatter named James White, who arrived sometime after the conclusion of the Creek War and, finding no one to tell him otherwise, decided to settle there. With statehood, almost overnight this serene riverside plain became the epicenter of government activities in one of the fastest-growing and ambitious states in the union. The city's development proved correspondingly rapid. The earliest known references to the town as an actual community did not appear until the summer of 1819, but by 1821 it ranked as one of the largest cities in the state and vibrated with activity. Along its spacious streets stood several inns: taverns; grocery, dry goods, and hardware stores; numerous lawyers' and doctors' offices; and the offices of two newspapers. In the heart of the town, physically and symbolically, stood the statehouse, constructed by David and Nicholas Crocheron. A large but rather unostentatious two-story cupola-topped brick structure, it served as Cahawba's reason for existence and became the epicenter of political power in the state.[8]

Depiction of the capitol at Cahawba, by Dr. Robert Mellown. Courtesy of the artist.

Cahawba's brief period as state capital paralleled the two terms of office of Governor Israel Pickens, one of early Alabama's most active and popular leaders. Governor Thomas Bibb, who preceded him, never could shake the perception among legislators that the mild-mannered executive was more a caretaker than a leader, nor did he appear to try very hard to disprove them. Consequently, the legislature passed little substantive legislation during the year he filled out his brother's term in office. In contrast, Pickens proved to be an activist who would bring fundamental change to Alabama's political infrastructure and tackle some of its most pressing issues.[9]

Israel Pickens moved to Alabama from his native North Carolina, where he had served in the state legislature and as a representative in the United States Congress, in 1817. During service as a land registrar in Saint Stephens and later as the first president of the Tombeckbe Bank, he won a reputation

Governor Israel Pickens. Courtesy of the Alabama Department of Archives and History.

as a capable administrator and energetic leader in his new home, which he parlayed into a successful bid for the governorship in 1821. Although affiliated with the Georgia faction as he entered Alabama politics, Pickens rose to statewide prominence for his stance against the elite groups' concentration of power as resentment against it mounted in the wake of the setbacks of the Panic of 1819. His populist appeal as a champion of the common man not only won him election to the state's highest office but also sparked a sea change in Alabama's political landscape that finally ended the days of Royal Party rule and ushered in a new era of more democratic campaigning by candidates for office. Following his example, in which he twice defeated Georgia-faction-backed Dr. Henry Chambers by large margins, office seekers would henceforward court voters more directly by stressing their shared concerns.[10]

During his two terms as governor, Pickens oversaw the establishment of much of the infrastructure of the young state. Foremost among the major issues on his agenda in this regard stood the establishment of a state university and a state bank, unexpectedly related causes to which Pickens devoted a significant portion of his time and effort. The untimely death of his wife and one of his children a short time after his reelection in 1823 made it possible for him to exert more time and effort toward the issues on his agenda. He immersed himself in his job thereafter, consuming his time with political affairs perhaps in part to escape his grief. Pickens strongly believed Alabama needed a state-run bank after seeing how mismanagement of the privately owned Planters and Merchants Bank during the recent depression had advantaged the wealthy and devastated so many common citizens. His efforts to have the bank resume specie payment after the disaster directly hastened its demise, and he pushed for a state institution to take its place. Through skillful political maneuvering, Pickens persuaded legislators to move to sell lands set aside to support the creation of the University of Alabama (authorized by the legislature in 1820) but invest a portion of the proceeds in his bank project rather than in actual construction while debate over selection of a campus site took place. With these critical funds and the sale of state bonds and federal land grants, the bank opened in 1824 and soon became a critical and stabilizing influence in the economic life of the state. The university would eventually be located in Tuscaloosa in 1827 and open in 1831. So successful had Pickens been during his tenure of office that his hand-picked successor, fellow North Carolinian John Murphy, succeeded him as governor for two terms beginning in 1825, both times running unopposed.[11]

The state Murphy would govern would be much more involved in national politics than it had been during Pickens's administrations. The rise of Jacksonian democracy, essentially the creation of a national political party around the personality of military hero Andrew Jackson, heavily influenced local politics as early as the mid-1820s. Jackson's appeal to the common man and wholehearted endorsement of what historians now call the concept of Manifest Destiny, construed in the South to mean, in immediate terms, the removal of any native groups that stood in the way of the expansion of American settlement and a full-throated endorsement of the rights of slaveholders, withered political rivals in emerging states for a time. Within just a few years, support or opposition to Jackson's policies would become the de facto litmus test of political loyalty in many quarters of Alabama and would transform the state's early loose alliances into actual party affiliations either in favor of, or, later,

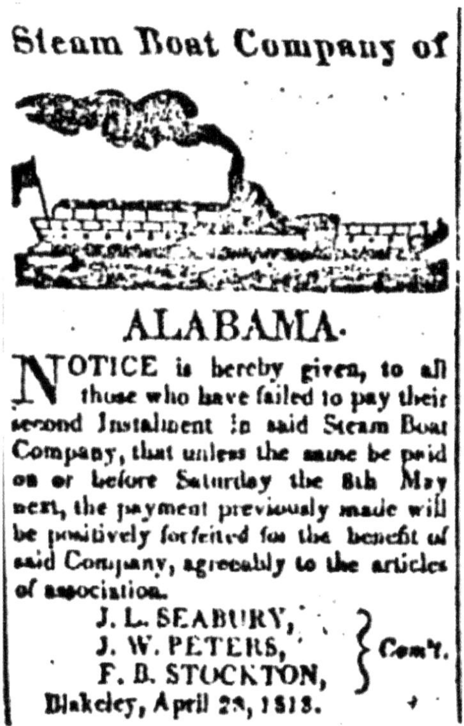

Steam Boat Company of

ALABAMA.

NOTICE is hereby given, to all those who have failed to pay their second Instalment in said Steam Boat Company, that unless the same be paid on or before Saturday the 8th May next, the payment previously made will be positively forfeited for the benefit of said Company, agreeably to the articles of association.

J. L. SEABURY,
J. W. PETERS,
F. B. STOCKTON, } Com'r.

Blakeley, April 28, 1818.

Image from a notice by the Steamboat Company of Alabama that appeared in the *Blakeley Sun*. Courtesy of Historic Blakeley State Park.

pitted against his influence. Both houses of the state legislature passed resolutions endorsing Jackson as a "suitable candidate for the President of the United States" in 1824. In his contest with John Quincy Adams, Jackson that year carried the majority of all but three counties in the state. By the latter part of the decade, Alabama had become in many respects a single-party state.[12]

The Alabama of Murphy's administration had also become dramatically more interconnected than it had been when his predecessor took office. In the early 1820s officials authorized the construction or improvement of numerous roads crisscrossing the state, gradually making travel by land easier and more predictable as well as facilitating the advent of several stagecoach lines and spurring the placement of ferries wherever major roads intersected navigable streams. Steamboats, however, had truly revolutionized transportation of people and goods within the state in amazingly short order. The first boat to be built in the state, the *Alabama*, had been launched into the Tombigbee in February 1818 by the Saint Stephens Steamboat Company, and within the next year and a half pioneer builders at Blakeley had launched the *Mississippi* and the *Tensa*. The *Tensa* made its way from Mobile Bay to Cahawba in 1820. In the fall of that year the age of effective steamboat travel in the state officially began, as the *Harriet* successfully reached Montgomery after an uninterrupted ten-day voyage from Mobile. Prior to steamboats, transporting goods between those two points on flatboats or keelboats could often take at least two weeks going downriver, and twice that or more in the opposite direction. By 1825 about fifteen steamers navigated Alabama's waters, making in mere days regular round-trip journeys from interior ports to its gulf outlet at Mobile, or even from the Tennessee Valley to New Orleans, which connected producers and travelers far from the rivers' banks through a series of convenient landings. Alabama's early steamboats were a far cry from the floating palaces of river travel's heyday a generation later—primarily sidewheelers, which were slower, smaller, and far less powerful and reliable than those of the future—but they marked the beginning of the era of riverine transportation that lay at the core of Alabama's ascendance to become a key cog in the international antebellum cotton trade.[13]

Perhaps nothing more clearly signaled Alabama's arrival on the national scene than the visit of famed Revolutionary War hero Marie-Joseph Paul Yves Roch Gilbert du Motier, Marquis de Lafayette. A native of France born into that nation's aristocracy, Lafayette had volunteered to serve in the American army during its struggle for independence from Britain nearly half a century prior. Through his exploits engineering victory alongside George Washington, the young leader—only twenty at the time of his commissioning as a major general in 1777—had secured himself a place in America's pantheon of heroes. His fame among Americans only heightened as he subsequently became involved in the French Revolution and held various positions in the French government, always appearing a champion of the ideals on which America had been founded. In 1825 he ranked as somewhat of a living legend to many Americans, at least in part because so few of his contemporaries from the ranks of the Continental Army's officers survived at the time. President James Monroe invited Lafayette to visit the United States in 1824 in part to help celebrate the upcoming fiftieth anniversary of American independence. From August 1824 through September 1825 he and a small party, including his son Georges Washington, his aide Auguste Levasseur, and his faithful dog Quiz, conducted an epic grand tour of the United States in which the hero traveled over six thousand miles and visited every state. At virtually every stop, communities

The Marquis de Lafayette. Courtesy of the Library of Congress.

rolled out the red carpet for what they viewed as the biggest event in their history. Alabama provided as warm a welcome as it could, and then some, as in the final account it spent about a fifth of the entire state budget for 1825 on entertaining Lafayette.[14]

Lafayette entered Alabama's eastern border along the Chattahoochee near Fort Mitchell on March 31, 1825. The welcoming party consisted of something of a cross section of early Alabama society, including political dignitaries such as Revolutionary War veteran, former congressman, and planter Bolling Hall; frontiersman, Creek War veteran, and state legislator Sam Dale; former aid to Lafayette and current superintendent of the nearby Asbury School and Mission among the Creeks, the Reverend Isaac Smith; prominent Creek leader and son of legendary chieftain William McIntosh, Chilly McIntosh; and a group of state militiamen and a large number of Creek Indians, among others. Once Lafayette had crossed the river, Creeks carried their esteemed guest on a litter up the riverbank, where fantastically outfitted warriors greeted him with piercing war whoops. They later entertained him with one of the most elaborate displays of the "ball game"—the traditional Creek athletic contest known as the "little brother of war," the forerunner of modern stickball—to have been recorded. It was a magnificent sight that Lafayette's companion Levasseur detailed in his journal of the trip as one of the more remarkable scenes the traveling party had the pleasure to witness in America.[15]

Lafayette's party then made its way westward through Creek territory into Alabama's American-settled interior, stopping at taverns and inns alongside the Federal Road before arriving at Montgomery on April 3. Governor Pickens provided an official welcome address to the travelers there, and a grand public celebration, serenaded by a band from New Orleans, ensued. Lafayette continued along the Alabama River aboard a steamboat from there, making a brief stop at Selma before docking at Cahawba on April 5. He entered the capital city under an elaborate decorative arch as a band played "Lafayette's March." During his stay in Cahawba local citizens feted Lafayette with a reception at the new statehouse and hosted two dinners—a formal one for invited dignitaries and a more casual one that the general public attended. Levasseur remembered the entertainment provided as "remarkable for their elegance and good taste, as touching by their cordiality and the feelings of which they were the expression." From Cahawba the general continued downriver to Claiborne, stopping for a few hours to attend a reception that included a feast featuring "6 hams, 8 roast turkeys, 6 roast pigs, 24 fowls, 12 ducks, 6 dishes of roast beef, 8 dishes of mutton and kid with the necessary trimmings, vegetables, pastry, and coffee." After being feted at another large ball in Mobile, his journey in Alabama concluded at Mobile Point on April 8, where he boarded a steamer bound for the Mississippi.[16]

Lafayette's visit had seemed to cause a suspension in partisan squabbling in Cahawba, but shortly after his departure it resumed on the biggest of issues in early Alabama politics. The 1818 legislation, which had designated Cahawba as the state capital, had essentially called for a referendum on the matter by 1825, and as the time for a vote approached, change appeared imminent. Cahawba had not been the choice of a majority of south or north Alabama's leaders, and its temporary designation as the state's seat of government required compromise arrangements that left its role inherently fragile. In truth, legislators, editors, and others unhappy with the capital city had looked to discredit it at every turn. Detractors exaggerated Cahawba's periodic flooding and general unhealthiness, in the process giving rise to the entirely fabricated but still persistent legend of legislators rowing into a second-story window to conduct business during a period of high water on the Cahawba and Alabama Rivers. The fact that yellow fever struck the town in 1821 did nothing to help its cause and only gave more ammunition to those who wanted to relocate the capital.[17]

By the time of the vote on the issue in the winter of 1825, many believed the removal of the capital from Cahawba to be a foregone conclusion. Its best chance of keeping its title appeared to lay in the fact that those who desired the seat of government to remain in the Alabama River region failed to coalesce around a single proposed alternative location, leaving open the possibility that no consensus on a new site might be reached and Cahawba would continue as the capital by default. Its fate was sealed. When legislators voted on the issue on December 13, 1825, they chose to designate Tuscaloosa as the next capital of Alabama.[18]

Tuscaloosa seemed a natural spot for connecting north and south Alabama. Its location along the Black Warrior River—a stream the nationally distributed *Niles Weekly Register* in 1819 called the "Nile of the Western Country"—approximately equidistant from the gulf and the Tennessee River Valley, made it a strategic point in much of the travel and trade between the regions. It had, after all, been the presumed choice of a capital location before Governor Bibb found a way to circumvent the legislature in his efforts on behalf of Cahawba in 1818. In truth, though, Tuscaloosa in 1825 may have had little more claim to urban sophistication than Bibb's cherished planned city had in 1819. As late as 1817 a visitor described it as merely a "rude cluster of log huts, heterogeneously arranged, with little regard to regularity as to streets," and even in 1820 William Ely, an investor in the town, summed it up as merely "20 stores & little Groceries, or Hucksters Shops." Ely further disparaged the community in general, decrying "what they call their houses, are either the most despicable rough dirty & uncomfortable rolling log cabins, or less durable & more mean buildings; most of them without a single Pane of Glass, with scarcely a saw'd board or Plank, Nail or any other Iron about them." Nevertheless, by the time the legislature voted to move the state capital there, Tuscaloosa and the adjacent settlement of Newtown were moving toward consolidation into one of Alabama's larger communities.[19]

Alabama's legislature first gathered in its new capital city on November 20, 1826. As the construction of a statehouse took some time to accomplish, the body assembled at rented quarters for the next three years. It first met at the

Painting of the state capitol building in Tuscaloosa, ca. 1840, by Margaret Cammer Furman. Courtesy of W. S. Hoole Special Collections, the University of Alabama Libraries.

Bell Tavern and later at a larger rented building a few blocks away on Broad Street, before the completion of William Nichols's grand capitol building on a hill overlooking the Black Warrior. From within that structure Alabama's leaders would oversee two decades of steady growth and development as the state transitioned from unpolished frontier to one of the wealthiest and most influential states in the union.[20]

EPILOGUE

After the move of the capital to Tuscaloosa it would be nearly two decades before legislators would again contemplate relocating Alabama's seat of government, this time in response to economic and demographic shifts that could be traced back to the state's founding era. The slavery-based economic system on which the state in large part had been built was approaching its antebellum zenith in the mid-1840s when the move came under discussion. By then Alabama's rich central plantation belt had emerged as its paramount political and financial nerve center. The city of Montgomery, by then one of the largest communities in the state, also lay even more centrally located than Tuscaloosa in terms of population distribution at the time.

Even if Tuscaloosa may not have been destined to become quite as permanent a capital city as some might have assumed in 1825, its tenure as the state's seat of government marked the transition from Alabama's period of coalescence into a period of stability for a region that had long been characterized by uncertainty. In the seven years prior to the legislature's assembling on the Black Warrior, Alabama's capital had been rotated among four cities and its citizens forced to weather a series of political, economic, and military crises as they worked to establish the state. As recently as a dozen years previous, the state had been an overlooked portion of a sparsely populated territory in the throes of a destructive war and riven with international intrigue. Tuscaloosa would thus serve as the state's political center during a period of relatively steady growth and development approximately as long as Alabama's entire territorial saga. It would not be all peaceful or progressive by any means; the further entrenchment of slavery in Alabama, the brief but bloody Second Creek War (1836–37), and the tragic saga of Indian Removal were among the most unfortunate occurrences that marred its course over those years. But even these events worked to only accelerate the growth of the state, as they provided labor and land for an economy that drew its sustenance from both. At the time of Tuscaloosa's selection as capital, Alabama's population hovered around 150,000; it would reach 300,000 in 1830 and nearly 600,000 by 1840. By the time of the outbreak of the Civil War in 1861, the number of inhabitants approached an astounding one million and the state had become a regional economic powerhouse to a degree its founders probably could scarcely have imagined despite their optimism.[1]

Even at the time, Alabama's tumultuous journey from backwoods province to dynamic part of the American union charted with unrivaled clarity the course of the rise of the country's southwestern frontier to become its southern heartland. Alabama stood at the very center of that transition. So remarkable and swift had been its arrival on the national stage that the story of its becoming eclipsed other stories in the eyes of those interested in its past for a time. No less a historian than Albert James Pickett ended his famous 1851 *History of Alabama* with statehood, viewing that which came after too recent and too uninteresting to chronicle. With the establishment of the state, he seemed to imply, the die had been cast for all that would follow, and most events worthy of notice by historians had already taken place. With a touch of resignation, he wrote that "to some other person fonder than we are of the dry details of state legislation and fierce party spirit, we leave the task of bringing the history down to a later period." Obviously, in the century and a half that has passed since Pickett penned those thoughts, a lot has occurred that spectacularly belie his sentiment. We recognize a host of events that have transpired since the movement of the capital to Tuscaloosa as profoundly important in determining the trajectory of Alabama's continuing saga, sometimes to the inadvertent exclusion or downplaying of that formative era. Plus, if history teaches us anything, it is that individual decisions determine the course of events, and inevitability is a shaky notion by which to understand why things happened the way they did.[2]

But there remains an unmistakable element of truth in Pickett's dim assessment of things since the establishment of the state that continues to resonate today. In recognizing the land's potential and seeking to realize it in the fashion they did, Alabama's pioneers gave birth to a special society in terms of social custom and use of the physical environment that is inextricably linked to all that later rose from the foundation they laid. By the 1820s the lines along which Alabama would develop long had been, for better or worse, in great part well established. That heritage is directly linked to so many of the landmark events in Alabama's ensuing historical pageant—Indian Removal, the Civil War, the struggle for civil rights for its black citizens among the most prominent—that it is difficult to appreciate how Alabama's story has unfolded without a grasp of the overarching significance of its formative era.

HISTORIC SITES TOUR

The historic sites listed here, including museums, parks, homes, commercial and public buildings, and cemeteries, are some of the most significant locations associated with Alabama's territorial and early statehood era. Because the region that became Alabama originally lay within the Mississippi Territory, a few selected relevant sites in Mississippi, especially in the Natchez area, are included. While not a complete listing of historic sites associated with the era, it does include the great majority of publicly accessible sites and structures of interest to those wishing to learn more about the time period. Several of the extant private homes dating to the era are listed on this tour; they are marked as such and may only be viewed from nearby public streets. A selected few historic markers are also included. For a listing of historic markers statewide in Alabama visit https://www.alabamahistory.net/historical-markers.

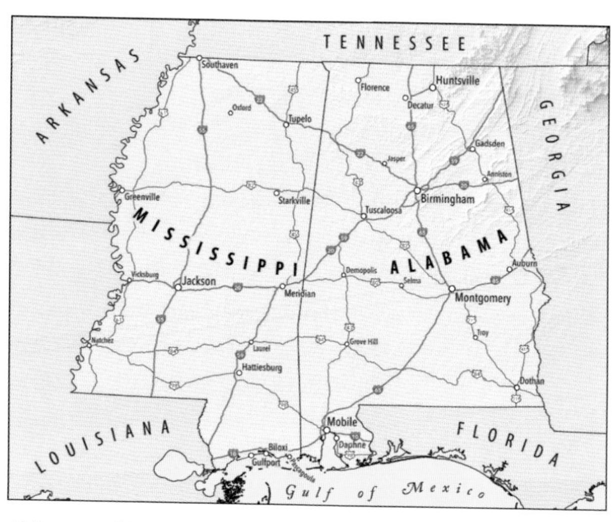

Alabama and Mississippi.

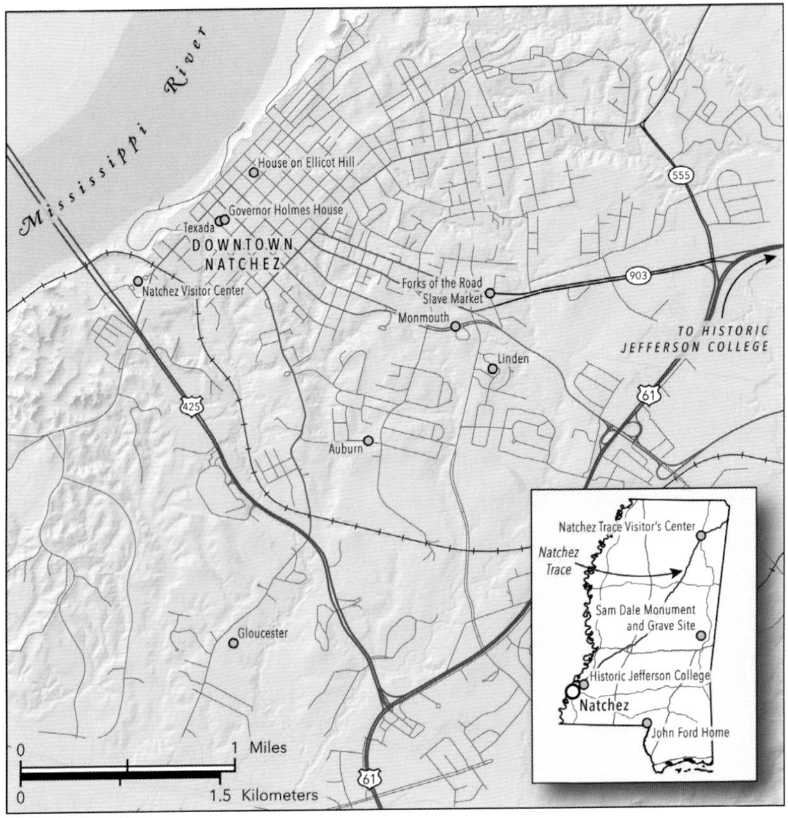

Natchez.

Mississippi River at Natchez. Photograph by Mike Bunn.

MISSISSIPPI

Natchez

Scenic Natchez, perched along a bluff overlooking the mighty Mississippi River, contains several historic sites significant to Alabama's territorial period. The city ranked as by far the largest and most sophisticated in the Mississippi Territory for most of its existence and served as the center of a great deal of its economic and political activity. Natchez and the nearby village of Washington—six miles from downtown—served as the headquarters of territorial government between the Mississippi Territory's formation in 1798 and its division in 1817.

Natchez Visitor Center
(640 South Canal Street, Natchez, MS)

A combination of a welcome center and interpretive center, the Natchez Visitor Center is recommended as the first stop for visitors to the city. In addition to exhibits and a film about the history of the town, it is where tickets to Natchez's many historic homes may be purchased and information on numerous other attractions found. http://visitnatchez.org/.

Governor Holmes House
(207 South Wall Street, Natchez, MS)

David Holmes, last governor of the Mississippi Territory and first governor of the state of Mississippi, lived here. The home was built in 1794 and is one of the few surviving structures from Natchez's colonial days. *Private residence.*

Texada
(222 South Wall Street, Natchez, MS)

Construction of Texada began circa 1793. The structure is believed to be the oldest brick building in Natchez. The house served as the capitol for the state of Mississippi from 1818 to 1820. *Private residence.*

House on Ellicott Hill. Photograph by Mike Bunn.

Auburn. Photograph by Mike Bunn.

House on Ellicott Hill
(211 North Canal Street, Natchez, MS)

Construction began on this house in 1798. It stands on the hill overlooking the Mississippi River made forever famous by Andrew Ellicott's raising of the American flag in defiance of Spanish attempts to delay their withdrawal from the region following their cession of the area in the Treaty of San Lorenzo. http://www.natchezpilgrimage.com.

Auburn
(400 Duncan Avenue, Natchez, MS)

Built in 1812 by the Mississippi Territory's attorney general Lyman Harding, Auburn is a National Historic Landmark. The home is credited with influencing the design of numerous homes across the South. http://auburnmuseum.org/.

Monmouth
(1358 John A. Quitman Boulevard, Natchez, MS)

Built in 1818, Monmouth is most closely associated with political figure John A. Quitman, who bought the home in 1824 and lived there the remainder of his life. It is currently a bed and breakfast. http://www.monmouthhistoricinn.com/.

Gloucester
(201 Lower Woodville Road, Natchez, MS)

One of the best examples of Federal architecture in Mississippi, Gloucester was built about 1803 and was the home of the Winthrop Sargent, first governor of the Mississippi Territory. *Private residence.*

Linden
(1 Connor Circle, Natchez, MS)

Among the oldest homes in Natchez, the central portion of this mansion dates to the late 1700s while the east wing was constructed in 1818. The home is currently a bed and breakfast. http://www.lindenbandb.com/.

Site of Forks of the Road Slave Market. Photograph by Mike Bunn.

Several other homes in Natchez date to the territorial and early statehood era and are, on occasion, open to the public as part of the spring and fall Natchez Pilgrimage. For a current listing, visit www.natchezpilgrimage.com.

Forks of the Road Slave Market
(Intersection of D'Evereaux Drive, Liberty Road,
and Saint Catherine Street, Natchez, MS)

This outdoor park, located on the site of one of the South's largest slave markets, interprets its history and the larger story of the slave trade in the region.

Historic Jefferson College
(16 Old North Street, Natchez, MS)

The first institution of higher learning chartered in the Mississippi Territory (1802), Jefferson College opened in 1811. The historic site today features a museum and several buildings dating to the 1830s. The East Wing was constructed in 1819. http://mdah.state.ms.us/new/visit/historic-jefferson-college/.

Near the entrance to the Historic Jefferson College historic site is a monument commemorating the Mississippi Constitutional Convention of 1817.

Historic Jefferson College. Photograph by Mike Bunn.

The convention met a few hundred yards away at a Methodist Church that no longer stands, and the state's first legislature convened nearby at DeFrance's Tavern, also known as Assembly Hall. That structure was destroyed in a fire in the 1990s, but the ruins of the structure's foundation still stand near the intersection of Highway 61 and Assembly Street. The site is owned by the Mississippi Department of Archives and History.

Sites in Mississippi outside of Natchez associated with Alabama's territorial years include:

Natchez Trace Visitor's Center
(2680 Natchez Trace Parkway, Tupelo, MS)

The Visitor's Center contains several exhibits about the trace and its history and is the primary stop for information on its many attractions. Along the route of the trace between Natchez and the Tennessee border are numerous points of historical interest, including *Mount Locust Inn and Plantation* (milepost 15.5), the oldest remaining inn on the trace, and the *Site of the Ferry Operated by George Colbert* (milepost 327.3). https://www.nps.gov/natr/index.htm.

Sam Dale Monument and Grave Site
(Hwy. 39, 15 miles north of Meridian, Daleville, MS)

Frontiersman, soldier, and politician, Sam Dale ranks as one of the most influential and colorful characters from Alabama's territorial and early statehood years. Dale saw action in several engagements of the Creek War, subsequently serving in the Alabama territorial and state legislatures. He spent his last years in Mississippi.

John Ford Home
(142 John Ford Home Road, Sandy Hook, MS)

Built around 1800 by frontier minister John Ford, this home was the site of the famous Pearl River Convention in October 1816. The assembly gathered to discuss whether the Mississippi Territory should move toward statehood as one or two states and resulted in the selection of a delegate, Judge Harry Toulmin, being sent to the nation's capital to lobby for its position. The home is owned and managed by the Marion County Historical Society and is open by appointment (601-731-3999).

ALABAMA

Mooresville

Incorporated in 1818 by the Alabama Territorial Legislature, Mooresville is one of Alabama's most historic communities. The entire town is listed on the National Register of Historic Places. The small town contains several homes that date to the early statehood era and other structures, such as churches and its circa 1840 post office, which date to later in the antebellum period. http://www.mooresvilleal.com/.

The Stagecoach Inn and Tavern
(4936 High Street, Mooresville, AL)

Built around 1820, this tavern along the road connecting Mooresville and Huntsville at first also doubled as a post office. Today it serves as a museum and town hall.

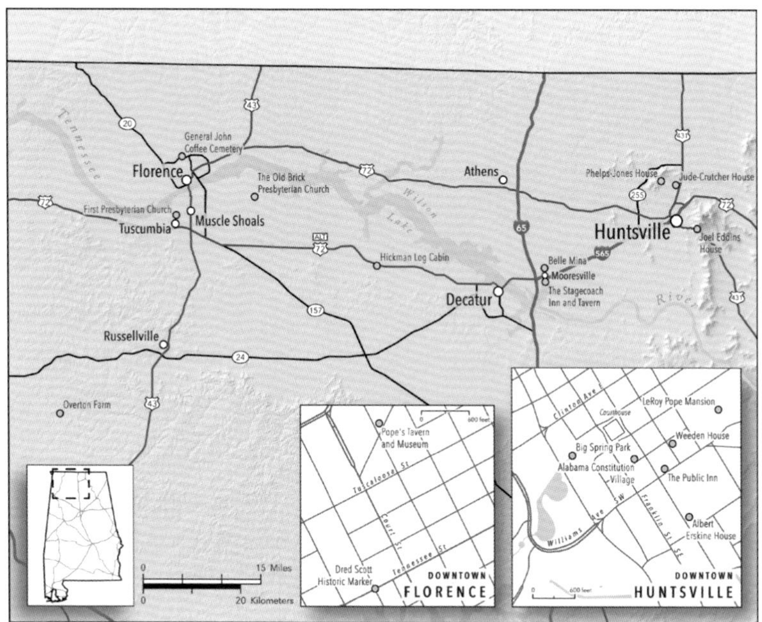

North Alabama.

The Stagecoach Inn and Tavern. Photograph by Mike Bunn.

Weeden House. Photograph by Mike Bunn.

A short distance from the heart of the town on Highway 71 (Mooresville Road) stands Belle Mina, the home of Governor Thomas Bibb. The circa 1826 home is privately owned, but a historic marker stands opposite it at 6185 Mooresville Road.

Huntsville

Alabama Constitution Village

(109 Gates Avenue SE, Huntsville, AL)

A living history museum interpreting life in early nineteenth-century Alabama, Constitution Village features several reconstructed historic structures available for a tour, including a law office, print shop, land surveyor's office, and post office. A reconstruction of the cabinet shop where the 1819 constitutional convention met stands at the corner of Gates and Franklin Streets. http://www.earlyworks.com/alabama-constitution-village/.

Weeden House
(300 Gates Avenue, Huntsville, AL)

Constructed in 1819 by Henry C. Bradford, the Weeden House is most closely associated with the family of Dr. William Weeden, who purchased the property in 1845. Today the home is a museum operated by the city of Huntsville; the museum interprets local history, especially the story of artist and poet Maria Howard Weeden. http://www.weedenhousemuseum.com/.

The Public Inn
(205 Williams Avenue SE, Huntsville, AL)

This rare Federal-period structure dates to 1818. Originally an inn in which some delegates to the 1819 constitutional convention are believed to have boarded, the building originally stood a few blocks away and was moved to its current location in the 1920s. Today it is a private home. A historic marker interpreting its history is located in front of the building.

Big Spring Park
(200 Church Street NW, Huntsville, AL)

Big Spring Park is the site of the natural limestone spring around which the community of Huntsville developed in the early 1800s. John Hunt, credited with founding the town, built his cabin on the bluff above the spring circa 1805. Running through the park are the remains of a canal built in the late 1820s to connect via water downtown Huntsville and the Tennessee River.

LeRoy Pope Mansion
(403 Echols Avenue, Huntsville, AL)

The oldest building in the city of Huntsville and possibly the oldest brick building in the state of Alabama, the Pope Mansion was constructed in 1814 by LeRoy Pope. Pope was an influential political figure in early Alabama and is recognized as a founder of modern Huntsville. The home remains a private residence, but a historic marker interpreting its history stands near the entrance to the property.

Joel Eddins House. Photograph by Mike Bunn.

Joel Eddins House
(Burritt on the Mountain, 3101 Burritt Drive, Huntsville, AL)

Built in 1808, the Eddins House is believed to be the oldest dwelling of any kind in the state of Alabama. The home originally stood near the community of Ardmore, north of Huntsville, but is now part of the collection of historic structures at Burritt on the Mountain, an educational park on Monte Sano Mountain overlooking Huntsville. http://www.burrittonthemountain.com/.

Numerous other private homes dating to the era stand in Huntsville, including:

Albert Erskine House
(527 Franklin Street)

Phelps-Jones House
(6112 Pulaski Pike)

Jude-Crutcher House
(2132 Winchester Road)

Pope's Tavern and Museum. Photograph by Mike Bunn.

Florence, Muscle Shoals, and Tuscumbia

Pope's Tavern and Museum
(203 Hermitage Drive, Florence, AL)

One of the oldest buildings in Florence, the tavern dates to at least the 1820s and is believed to have been built on the location of an earlier inn that predates the town's founding. Several modifications to the structure have taken place over the years. It is perhaps most famous for its use as a hospital during the Civil War. http://www.visitflorenceal.com/things_to_do/popes-tavern-and-museum/.

Dred Scott Historic Marker
(Intersection of North Pine Street and West Tennessee Street, Florence, AL)

Slave Dred Scott, whose name later became associated with the landmark 1857 decision by the US Supreme Court denying the citizenship of slaves, lived in Florence with the family of Peter Blow from 1820 to 1830.

First Presbyterian Church. Photograph by Mike Bunn.

General John Coffee Cemetery

(Off Surveyor Road across from the Cloverdale Road Walmart Supercenter, Florence, AL)

John Coffee, Creek War veteran, surveyor, planter, and cofounder of Florence, is buried in this family cemetery, located on what were once the grounds of his Hickory Hill plantation.

The Old Brick Presbyterian Church

(260 Mount Pleasant Road, Muscle Shoals, AL)

A National Historic Landmark, this church was dedicated in 1828. The congregation was formed in 1820.

First Presbyterian Church

(103 North Broad Street, Tuscumbia, AL)

One of the oldest churches in the state, this house of worship was erected in 1827.

Overton Farm cabin. Photograph by Mike Bunn.

Along Highway 20, connecting Decatur and Tuscumbia, is the:

Hickman Log Cabin

(Pond Spring, 12280 Highway 20, Hillsboro, AL)

A dogtrot cabin built in 1818, this building is located at Pond Spring, the plantation of General Joe Wheeler. It was built by the original owners of the property, the John P. Hickman family, shortly after their arrival. The plantation and grounds are operated as a house museum by the Alabama Historical Commission. https://ahc.alabama.gov/properties/pondspring/pondspring.aspx.

Southwest of Hillsboro, in the community of Hodges, is:

Overton Farm

(Overton Farm Road, off Highway 172 north of Hodges, AL)

About 1819, early settler Abner Overton built a log cabin on this spot, to which he gradually added rooms over the years as he operated a farm along Bear Creek. Only the double pen dogtrot cabin at the complex's core remains. The building underwent restoration in the 1970s and was later modified to serve as an educational center and then, later, as a restaurant. For access, call Rock Creek Canyon Equestrian Park (205-935-3499).

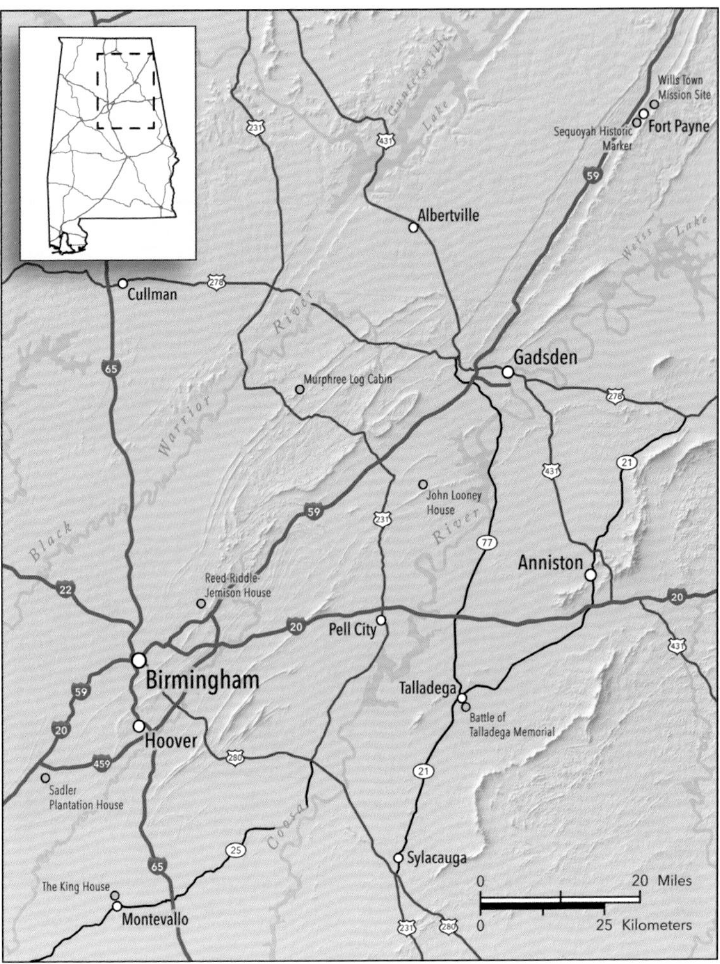

North central Alabama.

The King House

(Between Highland and King-Harman Streets across from the Carmichael Library, University of Montevallo, Montevallo, AL)

The King House, built in 1823 by Edmund King, is the oldest building on the University of Montevallo campus. Slaves constructed it using bricks made of clay from nearby Shoal Creek. In 1851 King donated land a short distance from his home for an academy. Eventually surrounded by the growth of the university, founded in 1896, the King House has served as a classroom and office building over the years. Today it serves the university as a guest house.

The King House. Photograph by Mike Bunn.

Sadler Plantation House

(Eastern Valley Road, McCalla, approximately a mile south of I-459 heading toward Tannehill State Park)

The core part of this historic home is a single pen log cabin constructed in 1817 by early settler John Loveless. According to oral tradition, Loveless built his cabin in an old Indian field shortly after arriving in the area from South Carolina. Later owners, the Sadler family, enclosed the structure with additions beginning in the 1830s. The grounds are open to the public. Tours of the interior of the structure can be arranged by contacting the West Jefferson County Historical Society (205-426-1633).

Murphree Log Cabin

(Palisades Park, 1225 Palisades Parkway, Oneonta, AL)

Daniel Murphree built this cabin a few miles north of the modern city of Oneonta about 1820. It stayed in the family's possession until the 1960s, when the last private owner donated it to the Blount County Historical Society. The society had it moved to Palisades Park in the 1970s.

Murphree log cabin. Photograph by Mike Bunn.

Reed-Riddle-Jemison House
(888 Twin Lakes Drive NE, Birmingham, AL)

Built circa 1816 in the Huffman area by William Reed, this cabin is believed to be the oldest dwelling within the city limits of Birmingham. The structure has been significantly altered and today forms the core of a modern private home.

Battle of Talladega Memorial
(Intersection of West Battle Street and South Spring Street, Talladega, AL)

The Battle of Talladega, fought on November 9, 1813, at the site of the Creek village of that name, was an important Creek War victory for Andrew Jackson's army. A memorial interpreting the battle stands downtown. A few blocks away on Spring Street stands Oak Hill Cemetery, believed to have been the site of a portion of the Creek village. A monument to Jackson's soldiers killed in the battle stands near the entrance to the cemetery.

John Looney House

(4187 Greensport Road, Ashville, AL)

Built between 1818 and 1820 by Creek War veteran and Tennessee native John Looney and his family, the Looney House is the oldest two-story dogtrot home in the state. One of the best examples of pioneer architecture in Alabama, it is listed on the National Register of Historic Places and operated as a historic house museum by the Saint Clair County Historical Society. The house and grounds are the site of the society's annual fall festival. Tours can be arranged by appointment (205-629-6897).

Sequoyah Historic Marker and the Wills Town Mission Site

(Fort Payne, AL)

Sequoyah, the noted inventor of the Cherokee alphabet, lived in a community called Wills Town, near modern Fort Payne, Alabama, between 1818 and 1823. During his stay he completed much of the work on developing a written language for his people. In 1823 the American Board of Missions authorized a mission to be established at Wills Town, which operated until the removal of the Cherokee in 1838. Historic markers for Sequoyah and the mission are located in City Park, on Gault Avenue North, between Fourth and Fifth Streets. Approximately three miles northeast on Thirty-Eighth Street NE near its intersection with Godfrey Avenue is a cemetery used by the Cherokee of Wills Town and the residents of the mission.

Montgomery

Old Alabama Town

(301 Columbus Street, Montgomery, AL; www.oldalabamatown.com)

Old Alabama Town is a collection of nineteenth-century buildings interpreted as a village in the heart of downtown Montgomery. Included along the tour are several structures associated with territorial and early statehood Alabama:

Lucas Tavern

(301 North Hull Street, Montgomery, AL)

Built circa 1818, the tavern is the oldest structure in Montgomery County. It was moved here from its original location along the Federal Road east of town

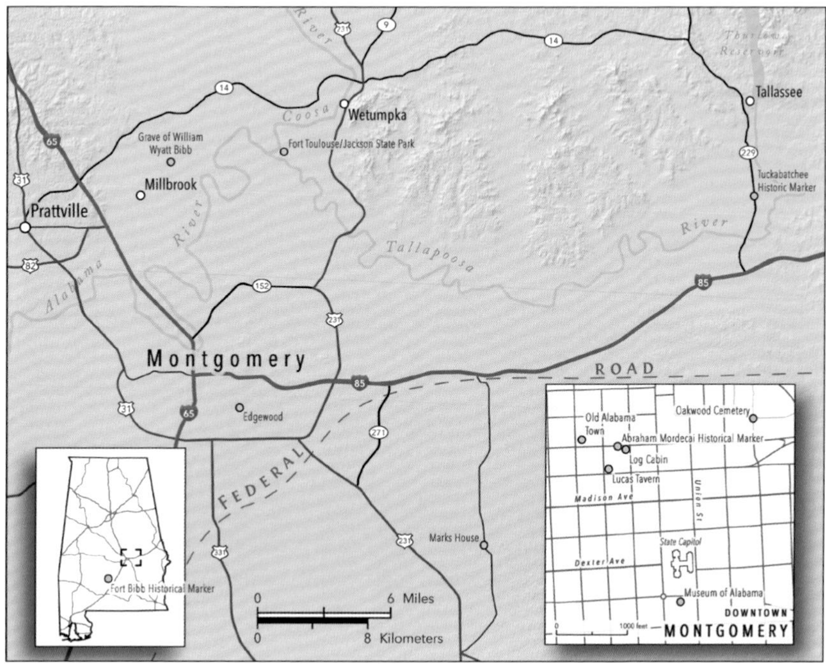

Central Alabama.

in the 1970s. A rare surviving example of roadside taverns, it hosted Lafayette during his visit to Alabama in 1825.

Log Cabin
(The "Living Block" of Old Alabama Town, Montgomery, AL)

Constructed about 1820 on a farm south of Montgomery and moved to its current site in the 1970s, this log cabin is an excellent example of the craftsmanship that went into the building of early settler homes. The single pen structure features logs joined by dovetail notching and "morning" and "afternoon" porches.

Abraham Mordecai Historic Marker
(nearby on Columbus Street, Montgomery, AL)

Believed to be the first American to settle in what became Montgomery County, Mordecai traded with the area Creek Indians and operated what is thought to be the first cotton gin in the state.

Lucas Tavern. Photograph by Mike Bunn.

Others sites of interest in Montgomery include:

Museum of Alabama
(624 Washington Avenue, Montgomery, AL)

The Museum of Alabama contains the state's largest and most comprehensive overview exhibits of its past from prehistory to the present day. The museum features several themed permanent galleries. The centerpiece exhibition, the award-winning *Alabama Voices*, chronicles Alabama's territorial and early statehood periods and showcases a number of rare artifacts from the era. www.museum.alabama.gov/.

Oakwood Cemetery
(829 Columbus Street, Montgomery, AL)

Perched on a scenic bluff overlooking the Alabama River valley, Oakwood Cemetery served as the primary burying place for early Montgomery and contains the graves of generations of prominent Alabamians.

Museum of Alabama. Courtesy of the Alabama Department of Archives and History.

Edgewood
(3175 Thomas Avenue, Montgomery, AL)

The oldest surviving original residence in Montgomery, Edgewood is a Federal-style home built in 1821; it was moved to its current location in the 1830s. *Private residence.*

A short drive outside of Montgomery are:

Grave of William Wyatt Bibb
(Auburn Road, off County Road 23, Coosada, AL)

William Wyatt Bibb served as the only governor of the Alabama Territory and as the first governor of the state of Alabama. He died after a fall from a horse in July 1820 and was buried in this small cemetery near his home (no longer standing). A historic marker with details about his life stands at the intersection of Auburn Road and County Road 23.

Grave of William Wyatt Bibb. Photograph by Mike Bunn.

Tuckaubatchee Historic Marker

(Highway 229 just outside of Tallassee, AL)

Tuckaubatchee was a major Creek population and political center located on the west bank of the Tallapoosa River just south of the modern city of Tallassee. The town hosted the Creeks' annual council where Tecumseh made his impassioned speech in September 1811 urging them to do whatever was necessary to recover their ancestral ways. A historic marker stands near the site of the town on the west side of Highway 229, approximately five miles north of I-85. An older stone monument commemorating the town stands in front of city hall on Freeman Avenue in Tallassee.

Fort Toulouse – Fort Jackson Park

(2521 West Fort Toulouse Road, Wetumpka, AL)

Site of a Mississippian-era Native American mound, a colonial-era French outpost, and the fortification at which the treaty ending the Creek War was negotiated, this park is located on a scenic bluff at the confluence of the Coosa and Tallapoosa Rivers. It features a reconstruction of the French fort and a partial reconstruction of Fort Jackson. https://fttoulousejackson.org/.

Marks House

(890 Old Carter Hill Road, Pike Road, AL)

This home was originally built by early settler William Matthews Marks. It has served the Pike Road area as a community center since the 1960s.

Farther south of Montgomery is:

Fort Bibb Historic Marker

(County Road 10 near Greenville, AL,
about twelve miles from exit 128 on I-65)

Fort Bibb, named after territorial governor William Wyatt Bibb, was one of several forts constructed in the Alabama Territory during conflicts with Creeks and Seminoles associated with the First Seminole War.

Fort Toulouse – Fort Jackson Park. Photograph by Mike Bunn.

The Federal Road

A path cleared in the first decade of the 1800s connected central Georgia with what is now southwest Alabama. It served as a primary immigration route for many American settlers during the territorial and early statehood period. The original route of the road, which roughly parallels Highway 80 running between Phenix City and Montgomery and Interstate 65 between Montgomery and Mobile, can be traced for short distances in several areas of east and south Alabama. Several modern roadways follow portions of the road. One of the longest and easiest-to-follow sections of the original road (nearly thirty miles), which for the most part corresponds with modern roads, can be found along the Conecuh-Monroe County border. Conecuh County Road 5 forms a long section of the border between the two counties. The paved section of County Road 5 running south from the community of Skinnerton (near the town of Midway, which is approximately twenty-five miles west of Georgiana along Interstate 65) to its intersection with Highway 84 follows closely the original route of the Federal Road for over twenty miles. From there, the county road continues to follow the original road south to near the Escambia County line. Portions of this section of the road are paved and others are dirt, however.

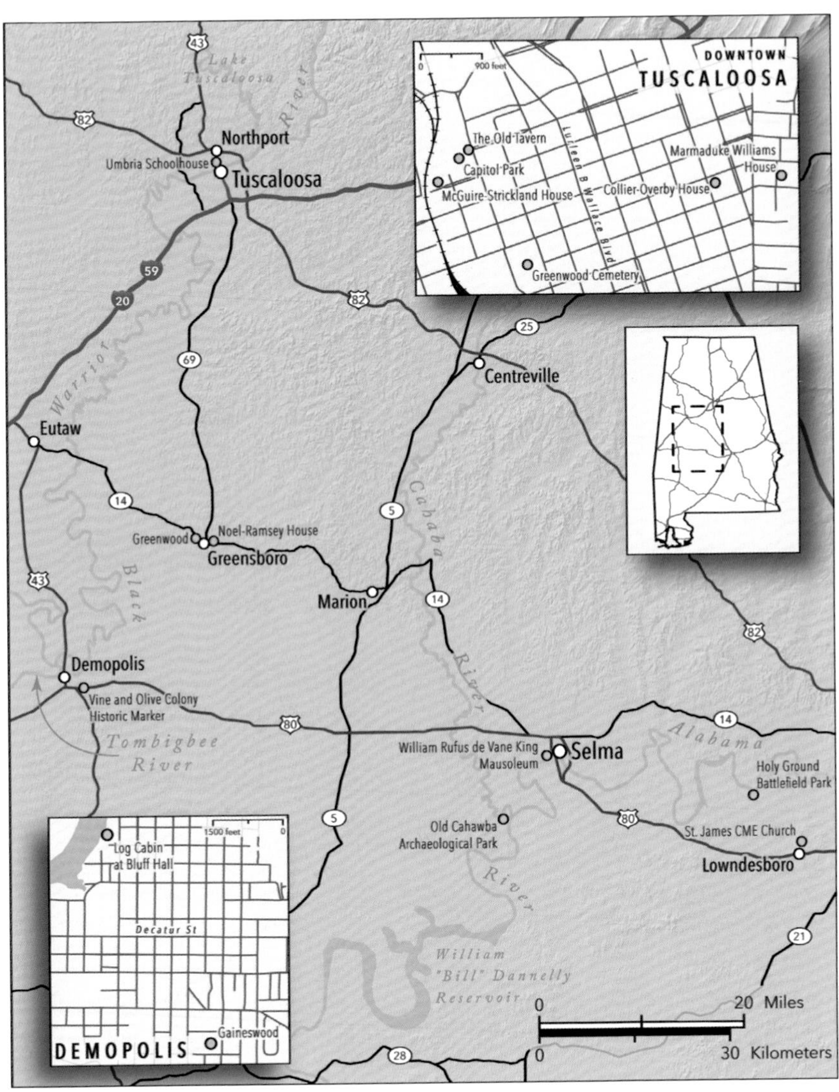

West central Alabama.

Log Cabin at Bluff Hall

(407 North Commissioners Avenue, Demopolis, AL)

Bluff Hall is a historic home built in 1832 and now operated as a museum. On Bluff Hall's grounds stands a log cabin believed to date to Demopolis's earliest American settlement. The cabin was discovered within the structure of a later house undergoing demolition in the 1980s and was moved to its current site. A

Log cabin at Bluff Hall. Photograph by Mike Bunn.

chimney and roof were added but most of the remainder of the structure dates to circa 1820. http://alabama.travel/places-to-go/bluff-hall.

Gaineswood
(805 South Cedar Avenue, Demopolis, AL)

Recognized as among Alabama's finest examples of Greek Revival architecture, Gaineswood has its origins in a dogtrot cabin constructed by longtime Choctaw Trading House factor George Strother Gaines. When builder Nathan Bryan Whitfield began construction of the home in 1843, he incorporated the 1821 cabin. A portion of the walls of the log structure remain on view today. https://ahc.alabama.gov/properties/gaineswood/gaineswood.aspx.

Vine and Olive Colony Historic Marker
(Eastern city limits of Demopolis along Highway 80 West, Demopolis, AL)

Demopolis traces its history to the French exiles of the Vine and Olive Colony, who settled in the area at the invitation of the United States government.

Although their experiment in growing grapes and olives as cash crops was a failure and most of the immigrants remained here only a short time, the colony is remembered as among Alabama's most famous early settler communities.

Old Cahawba Archaeological Park
(9518 Cahaba Road, Orrville, AL)

The park preserves the site of the ghost town of Cahawba, location of Alabama's first state capital. The town was laid out in 1819 and rose to become one of Alabama's leading trading centers before languishing in the latter half of the nineteenth century. The park features a visitor's center, an organized driving or hiking tour, ruins of several historic structures associated with the antebellum town, a small number of intact structures dating to the era of Cahawba's heyday, cemeteries, and scenic views of the confluence of the Cahaba and Alabama Rivers. The park also includes the site of a Civil War prison and the remnants of an earthen moat built by Native Americans who occupied a fortified village on the site over five hundred years ago. https://ahc.alabama.gov/properties/cahawba/cahawba.aspx.

Saint James CME Church
(South Broad Street, Lowndesboro, AL)

The copper-plated dome sitting atop this church is believed to be the sole surviving remnant of Alabama's capitol in Cahawba. It was moved here after the capitol fell into disuse following the removal of state government offices. The antebellum church (circa 1833) has served both white and black congregations over the years and is today used as a community center.

Holy Ground Battlefield Park
(300 Battlefield Road, Lowndesboro, AL)

The park is the site of an important Red Stick town and spiritual center that was destroyed by General Ferdinand Claiborne's army during the Creek War. It is perhaps best remembered as the location where noted chief William Weatherford, astride his horse Arrow, made his famous leap from the bluff into the Alabama River to escape advancing American forces. The park features a scenic overlook, picnic shelters, and playgrounds. Call the Alabama River Lakes Site Office, US Army Corps of Engineers, for hours of operation (334-872-9554). https://alabama.travel/places-to-go/holy-ground-battlefield-park.

Saint James CME Church. Photograph by Mike Bunn.

William Rufus de Vane King Mausoleum

(Off Dallas Avenue in Live Oak Cemetery, Selma, AL)

A founder of Selma, delegate to the Alabama constitutional convention, and US senator, King is most well known for his service as vice president of the United States in 1853.

Tuscaloosa

Capitol Park

(University Boulevard and Twenty-Eighth Avenue, Tuscaloosa, AL)

The park showcases the ruins of the Alabama capitol that stood here during Tuscaloosa's days as the state's seat of government. The cornerstone of the building was laid in 1827 and the first legislative assembly convened within its walls in 1829. After removal of the capital to Montgomery in 1847, the building served as the home of Alabama Central Female College until it burned in 1923. On view today are the original foundation of the building and a partial reconstruction of selected elements. Prior to construction of the capitol, the legislature met in Bell Tavern, which once stood at the intersection of University Boulevard and Twenty-Second Avenue, and a temporary wooden capitol that stood along Broad Street.

McGuire-Strickland House

(2828 Sixth Street, Tuscaloosa, AL)

Probably built in the 1820s, this home is believed to be one of the oldest wooden frame structures in Tuscaloosa County. Probate judge Moses McGuire was an early owner of the home, which at the time of construction stood a few blocks southeast of its current location. The home is currently used as the offices of the Capitol School.

The Old Tavern

(500 Twenty-Eighth Avenue, Tuscaloosa, AL)

The Old Tavern was constructed shortly after the state capital was moved from Cahawba to Tuscaloosa on a site a few blocks from its current location. It served as a tavern, hotel, and temporary home and meeting place of early state legislators throughout the city's tenure as the seat of government. Today it is a museum showcasing early Tuscaloosa history and is open by appointment. www.historictuscaloosa.org.

Collier-Overby House

(905 Twenty-First Avenue, Tuscaloosa, AL)

Constructed in the early 1820s by James Walker and in 1826 purchased by future governor Henry Collier, the home has undergone several modifications over the years. *Private residence.*

Marmaduke Williams House

(907 Seventeenth Avenue, Tuscaloosa, AL)

Although constructed in the 1830s, the Marmaduke Williams home is of note because it is a rare surviving example of Federal-style architecture in the central Alabama region and because it was the home of early state political figure Marmaduke Williams. Williams was a delegate to Alabama's constitutional convention and the runner-up in its first gubernatorial election.

The Old Tavern. Photograph by Mike Bunn.

Greenwood Cemetery
(Ninth Street and Twenty-Seventh Avenue SW, Tuscaloosa, AL)

Laid out shortly after Tuscaloosa's founding, Greenwood is the final resting place for many of the city's prominent citizens from the early statehood era. Noteworthy among its graves is the headstone for Solomon Perteat, an influential and unusually wealthy free black craftsman and businessman of the era who for many years was one of Tuscaloosa's most active real estate investors.

Umbria Schoolhouse
(Northport Community Center Park, 2100 Park Street, Northport, AL)

Believed to be the oldest existing school structure in the state of Alabama, this schoolhouse was built on the Umbria Plantation near Greensboro circa 1829. After a fire destroyed the plantation in 1973, the schoolhouse was donated to a local corporation and moved to Tuscaloosa. The Friends of Historic Northport brought the structure here and restored it in 2005.

Umbria Schoolhouse. Photograph courtesy of Rachel Dobson.

Noel-Ramsey House
(909 Market Street, Greensboro, AL)

The oldest home in Greensboro and believed to be the only surviving home built by an original settler of the Vine and Olive Colony, this house was constructed around 1820. It is now owned by the Historic Hale County Preservation Society.

Greenwood
(Intersection of Main Street and Cork Street, Greensboro, AL)

This 1856 Greek Revival house, known as Greenwood, incorporates materials from the home of Israel Pickens, third governor of Alabama. The original Greenwood stood a few miles south of Greensboro.

Horseshoe Bend National Military Park
(11288 Horseshoe Bend Road, Daviston, AL)

This tranquil historic park, located in a horseshoe-shaped bend in the Tallapoosa River, witnessed one of the most vicious battles ever fought on Alabama soil. On March 27, 1814, the culminating battle of Andrew Jackson's campaign

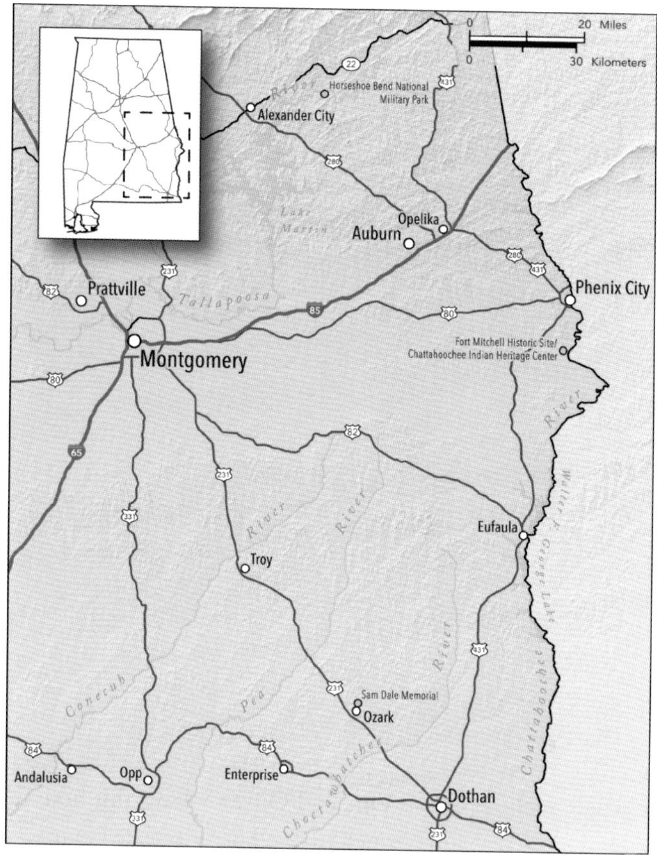

East Alabama.

Horseshoe Bend National Military Park. Photograph by Mike Bunn.

against the Red Stick Creeks raged on these grounds and effectively ended the Creek War. More Native Americans were killed here that day than at any other battle in US history. The park features driving and hiking tours of the battlefield and a visitor's center/museum. https://www.nps.gov/hobe/index.htm.

Fort Mitchell Historic Site and the Chattahoochee Indian Heritage Center
(561 Alabama Highway 165, Fort Mitchell, AL)

The site features a reconstruction of the 1813 fort that stood here, an early settler cabin moved to the grounds, a historic cemetery, and a museum and visitor's center. Adjacent to the park is the Chattahoochee Indian Heritage Center, an outdoor museum commemorating the Chattahoochee Valley's rich Native American heritage and the saga of Removal. http://alabama.travel/places-to-go/russell-county-historical-commission-historic-fort-mitchell.

Sam Dale Memorial
(Sam Dale Park and Ed Lisenby Public Lake, 861 Myrtle Drive, Ozark, AL)

This concrete memorial to Sam Dale, namesake of Dale County, Alabama, celebrates his life as a trader, soldier, and legislator in early Alabama. http://www.ozarkalabama.us/ozark/CityDepartments/LeisureServices/EdLisenbyLake/tabid/101/Default.aspx.

Mobile

History Museum of Mobile
(111 South Royal Street, Mobile, AL)

Showcasing the Mobile area's rich history, the museum features several permanent galleries and a regular schedule of temporary exhibits exploring the community's past. www.museumofmobile.com.

Fort Conde
(150 South Royal Street, Mobile, AL)

Fort Conde is a scale re-creation of the outpost originally built by the French founders of Mobile in 1723 and occupied for nearly a century after successively by the British, Spanish, and American armies. http://colonialmobile.com/.

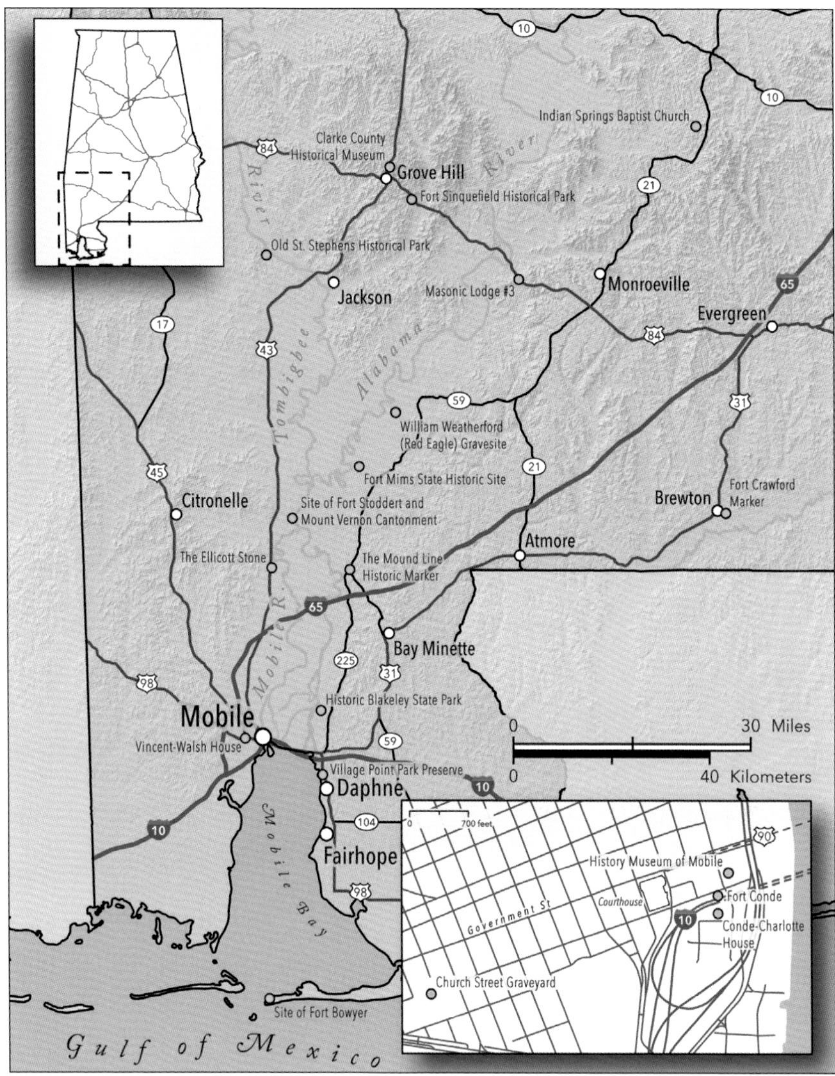

South Alabama.

Condé-Charlotte Museum

(104 Theatre Street, Mobile, AL)

Billed as the "Gateway to Mobile's History," the Condé-Charlotte House was built in 1850 on the foundation of the 1820s city jail. It interprets life in the city under French, English, Spanish, American, and Confederate rule. A portion of the original floor can be seen on house tours today. http://condecharlotte.com/.

Condé-Charlotte House. Photograph by Mike Bunn.

Church Street Graveyard
(Entrance beside Mobile Public Library on Scott Street, Mobile, AL)

With burials dating back to 1819, Church Street Graveyard is one of Mobile's oldest burying grounds. The cemetery contains the graves of early European settlers as well as Americans significant in early statehood history, including noted military leader Edmund Pendleton Gaines. Gaines at one point commanded nearby Fort Stoddert and arrested Aaron Burr. The cemetery is also the final resting place of Joe Cain, recognized as the founder of modern Mardi Gras in Mobile. http://www.cityofmobile.org/parks/churchstreetgraveyard.php.

Vincent-Walsh House
(1664 Springhill Avenue, Mobile, AL)

Built in 1827 by Captain Benjamin Vincent, the home is reputedly the oldest in Mobile. It currently houses the Mobile Medical Museum.
http://www.mobilemedicalmuseum.org/.

North of Mobile are:

The Ellicott Stone. Photograph by Mike Bunn.

The Ellicott Stone
(Highway 43 North in the vicinity of the community
of Bucks, AL, between mile markers 18 and 19)

This stone marker was placed April 10, 1799, by a crew led by Andrew Ellicott during the survey delineating the boundary between the Mississippi Territory and the Spanish colony of West Florida. The line Ellicott established remained the border between the United States and Spain in the region until its annexation by the United States during the War of 1812.

Site of Fort Stoddert and Mount Vernon Cantonment
(County Road 96, Mount Vernon, AL)

Built in 1799, Fort Stoddert served as a port of entry to the United States until the annexation of the Spanish colony of West Florida into the Mississippi Territory. The actual site of the fort on the Mobile River, near a public boat landing (three miles east of Highway 43) is unmarked, but its history is interpreted in the form of a history trail, historic markers relating the fort's history and that of closely related nearby Mount Vernon Cantonment, and a memorial to Mississippi Territory judge Ephraim Kirby. A mile west along County Road 96 stands the Mount Vernon Arsenal and Barracks, site of Mount Vernon Cantonment.

Historic Blakeley State Park. Photograph by Mike Bunn.

Gulf Coast and Eastern Shore

Site of Fort Bowyer

(Fort Morgan State Historic Site, Highway 180, Gulf Shores, AL)

Fort Bowyer, a War of 1812 fortification defending Mobile, stood on the site of Fort Morgan a generation prior to the famous Civil War Battle of Mobile Bay. It came under British assault twice during the conflict, in September 1814 and February 1815. While the majority of interpretation at Fort Morgan National Historic Landmark focuses on the Civil War era, interpretive panels explain its predecessor's significance. https://ahc.alabama.gov/properties/ftmorgan/ftmorgan.aspx.

Historic Blakeley State Park

(Highway 225, Spanish Fort, AL)

Site of one of early Alabama's largest cities, Blakeley is a 2,100-acre historical park along the Tensaw River preserving Native American, colonial era, and early American cultural heritage features. The park is most famous for being home to one of the nation's best-preserved Civil War battlefields (Battle of Fort Blakeley), as the site of the state's largest Civil War battle. www.blakeleypark.com.

Village Point Park Preserve

(27710 Main Street, Daphne, AL)

This approximately eighty-acre bayside park and nature preserve is located within the heart of a community dating to the colonial era known as The

Fort Mims State Historic Site. Photograph by Mike Bunn.

Village, forerunner of modern Daphne. Along its walking trails are an early settler cemetery and Jackson's Oak, one of the largest and oldest live oaks in the state. According to legend, General Andrew Jackson made a speech to his army from its limbs while marching between Pensacola and Mobile during the War of 1812. http://villagepoint.info.

Fort Mims State Historic Site

(Off County Road 80, Tensaw community north of Stockton, AL)

Fort Mims preserves the site of one of the most influential events in American history—the August 30, 1813, Battle of Fort Mims. It contains a reconstruction of the fort's walls, several interpretive panels, memorials to those who died there, and a small museum. https://ahc.alabama.gov/properties/ftmims/ftmims.aspx.

The Mound Line Historic Marker

(Highway 59 just north of intersection with Highway 225, Stockton, AL)

This marker stands near one of the last remaining earthen mounds marking the boundary between the Mississippi Territory and the Spanish colony of West Florida. The survey crew that delineated the boundary placed the mounds at intervals along portions of the border.

William Weatherford (Red Eagle) Gravesite

(T. J. Earle Road, off County Road 84,
Little River community north of Stockton, AL)

A small park contains the graves of Creek leader William Weatherford and his mother, Sehoy Tate Weatherford. Weatherford was an influential leader of Red Stick forces during the Creek War; he is credited with planning the attack on Fort Mims.

Washington and Clarke Counties

Old Saint Stephens Historical Park

(Off County Road 34, Saint Stephens, AL)

Site of the capital of the Alabama Territory, Saint Stephens hosted its two legislative sessions. It was once one of Alabama's largest cities. Today visitors can walk the original streets of Saint Stephens and discover where landmarks such as the Globe Hotel once stood. http://www.oldststephens.net/.

Fort Sinquefield Historical Park

(Fort Sinquefield Road, off Highway 84, Whatley, AL)

Interpreting the Creek War Battle of Fort Sinquefield, this small park stands on the site of a settler fort that came under attack by Red Sticks on September 2, 1813. It features several interpretive panels around the perimeter of the fort, a partial reconstruction of one of its walls, and a walking trail. A short distance

Old Saint Stephens Historical Park. Photograph by Mike Bunn.

away on the north side of Highway 84 stands a historic marker commemorating the Kimbell-James Massacre, an event that is closely related to the attack on Fort Sinquefield.

Clarke County Historical Museum
(116 West Cobb Street, Grove Hill, AL)

The Clarke County Historical Museum, housed in the Alston-Cobb House (1854), showcases exhibits relating to local history and hosts several special events throughout the year focusing on the frontier era. www.clarkemuseum.com.

Masonic Lodge #3
(Highway 84 and County Road 1 in Claiborne, AL)

The oldest building in Monroe County, the lodge was built in 1824 and has served many functions, including as a church and courthouse, over the years. Most famously, it served as the site of a reception for Lafayette during his visit to Alabama in 1825. Behind the lodge, facing Highway 84, is the Travis House (circa 1820), home of early Claiborne settler and, later, commander of the

Masonic Lodge #3. Photograph by Mike Bunn.

Alamo, William B. Travis. Approximately a mile west on a bluff overlooking the Alabama River stands a historic marker interpreting the early history of Claiborne and a stone monument commemorating the Creek War outpost named Fort Claiborne.

Also of note in the area are:

Indian Springs Baptist Church

(Highway 21 near the community of McWilliams in north Monroe County, AL)

Among the oldest wood-frame churches in the state, Indian Springs Baptist Church is believed to have been built as early as 1825. The church and associated cemetery stand along a dirt road 1.7 miles to the east of Highway 21 across from the historic marker.

Fort Crawford Marker

(Intersection of Shofner and Weaver Streets, East Brewton, AL)

Constructed in 1816 in an effort to curtail raids into the Mississippi Territory by former Red Stick Creeks and their Seminole allies in Florida in the years after the Creek War, Fort Crawford stood on a bluff overlooking Murder Creek, a tributary of the Conecuh River. The fort operated as an important base for operations against the Seminoles during the First Seminole War.

NOTES

CHAPTER ONE

1. The best study of the founding of Mobile is by Jay Higginbotham, *Old Mobile: Fort Louis de la Louisiane, 1702–1711* (Mobile: Museum of the City of Mobile, 1977). For an overview of Alabama's colonial years, the starting point remains Peter J. Hamilton, *Colonial Mobile: An Historical Study Largely from Original Sources, of the Alabama-Tombigbee Basin and the Old South West* (Boston: Houghton Mifflin, 1910). A more concise but authoritative summary of the colonial years can be found in William Warren Rogers et al., *Alabama: The History of a Deep South State* (Tuscaloosa: University of Alabama Press, 1994).

2. For information on Spain's Gulf Coast Campaign in the Revolutionary War, see Robert V. Haynes, *The Natchez District and the American Revolution* (Jackson: University Press of Mississippi, 1976); Jack D. L. Holmes, *Honor and Fidelity: The Louisiana Infantry Regiment and the Louisiana Militia, 1766–1821* (Birmingham: n.p., 1965); Albert Haarmann, "The Spanish Conquest of British West Florida, 1779–1781," *Florida Historical Quarterly* 39 (October 1960): 107–34. For information on Spain's withdrawal from the region, see Jack D. L. Holmes, "A Spanish Province, 1779–1798," in *History of Mississippi*, vol. 1, ed. Richard A. McLemore (Jackson: University of Mississippi Press, 1973), 158–73. For a detailed account of the Treaty of San Lorenzo el Real, consult Samuel Flagg Bemis, *Pinckney's Treaty: America's Advantage from Europe's Distress, 1783–1800* (New Haven, CT: Yale University Press, 1960).

3. *A Century of Lawmaking for a New Nation: U.S. Congressional Documents and Debates, 1774–1875, Statutes at Large*, 5th Congress, 2nd Session and 8th Congress, 1st Session, http://memory.loc.gov/ammem/amlaw/lawhome.html (accessed September 1, 2016), 549–50; Clarence Carter, ed., *The Territorial Papers of the United States*, vol. 5 (Washington, DC: Government Printing Office, 1937–38), 18–22, http://memory.loc.gov/ammem/amlaw/lawhome.html (accessed September 1, 2016), 303–5; George R. Lamplugh, "Yazoo Land Fraud," *New Georgia Encyclopedia*, http://www.georgiaencyclopedia.org/articles/history-archaeology/yazoo-land-fraud (accessed September 3, 2016).

4. Mike Bunn, "Spanish West Florida," *Encyclopedia of Alabama*, http://www.encyclopediaofalabama.org/article/h-3748 (accessed September 2, 2016). For an overview of the general unrest along the Mississippi Territory's border with Spanish West Florida and a detailed account of the West Florida Rebellion, see William C. Davis, *The Rogue Republic: How Would-Be Patriots Waged the Shortest Revolution in American History* (New York: Houghton Mifflin Harcourt, 2011); *Statutes*

at Large, 12th Congress, 1st Session, http://memory.loc.gov/ammem/amlaw/lawhome.html (accessed September 1, 2016), 734; and 15th Congress, 1st Session, 472; Lucille Griffith, *Alabama: A Documentary History to 1900* (Tuscaloosa: University of Alabama Press, 1987), 61–62; Melton McLaurin and Michael Thomason, *Mobile: The Life and Times of a Great Southern City* (Woodland Hills, CA: Windsor Publications, 1981), 24, 33.

5. Édouard de Montulé, *A Voyage to North America and the West Indies in 1817* (London: Sir Richard Phillips and Company, 1821), 93; Thomas D. Clark and John W. Guice, *Frontiers in Conflict: The Old Southwest, 1795–1830* (Norman: University of Oklahoma Press, 1989), 1–18.

6. James F. Barnett Jr., *Mississippi's American Indians* (Jackson: University Press of Mississippi, 2012), 165. For an overview of the background of the Natchez District, early Natchez, and Natchez-Under-the-Hill, see D. Clayton James, *Antebellum Natchez* (Baton Rouge: Louisiana State University Press, 1968); Noel Polk, ed., *Natchez before 1830* (Jackson: University Press of Mississippi, 1989); Holmes, "A Spanish Province," in McLemore, *A History of Mississippi*; Virginia Parks Matthias, "Natchez-Under-the-Hill: As It Developed under the Influence of the Mississippi River and the Natchez Trace," *Journal of Mississippi History* 7 (1945): 202–21; Edith W. Moore, *Natchez Under-the-Hill* (Natchez: Southern Historical Publications, 1958).

7. The best modern summary of the settlement of the Tensaw region is found in Gregory A. Waselkov, *A Conquering Spirit: Fort Mims and the Redstick War of 1813–1814* (Tuscaloosa: University of Alabama Press, 2006). Donna J. Siebenthaler, "Washington County," *Encyclopedia of Alabama*, http://www.encyclopediaofalabama.org/article/h-1295 (accessed September 4, 2016). For information on the history of Huntsville, see Edward Chambers Betts, *Early History of Huntsville, Alabama, 1804–1870* (Montgomery: Brown Printing, 1916); and Daniel S. Dupre, *Transforming the Cotton Frontier: Madison County, Alabama, 1800–1840* (Baton Rouge: Louisiana State University Press, 1997); Claire M. Wilson, "Abraham Mordecai," *Encyclopedia of Alabama*, http://www.encyclopediaofalabama.org/article/h-3135 (accessed September 4, 2016).

8. Westley F. Busbee Jr., *Mississippi: A History* (Wheeling, IL: Harland Davidson, 2005), 54; Carter, *Territorial Papers*, 5: 18–22; Robert V. Haynes, *The Mississippi Territory and the Southwest Frontier, 1795–1817* (Lexington: University Press of Kentucky, 2010), 27–69; Robert V. Haynes, "The Formation of the Territory," in *A History of Mississippi*, vol. 1, ed. Richard A. McLemore (Jackson: University and College Press of Mississippi, 1973), 174–216; John Wunder, "American Law and Order Comes to the Mississippi Territory: The Making of Sargent's Code, 1798–1800," *Journal of Mississippi History* 38 (1976): 132–33.

9. Haynes, *Mississippi Territory and the Southwest Frontier*, 48–69; Haynes, "Formation of the Territory," 196–202; Susanna Smith, "Washington, Mississippi: Antebellum Elysium," *Journal of Mississippi History* 40 (May 1978): 143–65; Junius P. Rodriguez, ed., *The Louisiana Purchase: A Historical and Geographical Encyclopedia* (Santa Barbara, CA: ABC-Clio, 2002), 70–71.

10. Haynes, *Mississippi Territory and the Southwest Frontier*, 85–88, 167–201; Haynes, "Formation of the Territory," 208–16; Franklin L. Riley, "Location of the Boundaries of Mississippi," *Publications of the Mississippi Historical Society* 3 (1900): 170; Carter, *Territorial Papers*, 5: 290, 297–98; Bunn, "Spanish West Florida"; Davis, *Rogue Republic*; Paul McWhorter Pruitt Jr., "Harry Toulmin," *Encyclopedia of Alabama*, http://www.encyclopediaofalabama.org/article/h-3108 (accessed September 5, 2016), and *Taming Alabama: Lawyers and Reformers, 1804–1929* (Tuscaloosa: University of Alabama Press, 2010), 1–13.

11. Stuart O. Stumpf, "The Arrest of Aaron Burr: A Documentary Record," *Alabama Historical Quarterly* 42 (Fall and Winter 1980): 113–23; David O. Stewart, *American Emperor: Aaron Burr's Challenge to Jeffersonian America* (New York: Simon and Schuster, 2011), 193–201.

12. Steven C. Hahn, "Creeks in Alabama," *Encyclopedia of Alabama*, http://www.encyclopediaofalabama.org/article/h-1088 (accessed September 6, 2016). There are several excellent studies

of the Creeks in Alabama. Among the most useful as it pertains to their history and occupation of Alabama during its territorial and early statehood periods are Kathryn E. Holland Braund, *Deerskins and Duffels: The Creek Indian Trade with Anglo-America, 1685–1815* (Lincoln: University of Nebraska Press, 1993); Robbie Ethridge, *Creek Country: The Creek Indians and Their World* (Chapel Hill: University of North Carolina Press, 2003); Michael D. Green, *The Politics of Indian Removal: Creek Government and Society in Crisis* (Lincoln: University of Nebraska Press, 1982); Steven C. Hahn, *The Invention of the Creek Nation, 1670–1763* (Lincoln: University of Nebraska Press, 2004); Claudio Saunt, *A New Order of Things: Property, Power, and the Transformation of the Creek Indians, 1733–1816* (New York: Cambridge University Press, 1999).

13. Among the most informative works in illuminating American interference in Creek life during the era are Ethridge, *Creek Country*; Braund, *Deerskins and Duffels*; and Benjamin Griffith Jr., *McIntosh and Weatherford: Creek Indian Leaders* (Tuscaloosa: University of Alabama Press, 1988). Critical to understanding American-Creek relations during the era are the writings of Creek agent Benjamin Hawkins, made available in edited volumes by Thomas Foster, *The Collected Works of Benjamin Hawkins, 1796–1810* (Tuscaloosa: University of Alabama Press, 2003); C. L. Grant, *Letters, Journals, and Writings of Benjamin Hawkins* (Savannah, GA: Beehive Press, 1980); and Merrit B. Pound, *Benjamin Hawkins, Indian Agent* (Athens: University of Georgia Press, 1951). See also Florette Henri, *The Southern Indians and Benjamin Hawkins* (Norman: University of Oklahoma Press, 1986); and Frank L. Owsley Jr., "Benjamin Hawkins, the First Modern Indian Agent," *Alabama Historical Quarterly* 30 (Summer 1968): 7–14. The most in-depth account of the Federal Road and the role it played in the history of the region through which it ran is Henry deLeon Southerland Jr. and Jerry Elijah Brown's *The Federal Road through Georgia, the Creek Nation, and Alabama, 1806–1836* (Tuscaloosa: University of Alabama Press, 1989). See also Angela Pulley Hudson, *Creek Paths and Federal Roads: Indians, Settlers, and Slaves and the Making of the American South* (Chapel Hill: University of North Carolina Press, 2010).

14. There are numerous and divergent accounts of Tecumseh's visit among the Southeastern Indians in 1811. Among the most informative are John Sugden, *Tecumseh: A Life* (New York: Henry Holt, 1997), 215–51; John Sugden, "Early Pan-Indianism: Tecumseh's Tour of the Indian Country, 1811–12," *American Indian Quarterly* (Fall 1986): 273–304; Benjamin Drake, *Life of Tecumseh, and His Brother the Prophet: With a Historical Sketch of the Shawnee Indians* (Cincinnati: E. Morgan, 1841), 141–45; George Stiggins, *Creek Indian History* (Birmingham: Birmingham Public Library Press, 1989), 83–96; Griffith, *McIntosh and Weatherford*, 69–78. An account of Tecumseh's speech at Tuckaubatchee "as recorded from eyewitness accounts," which first appeared in J. F. H. Claiborne's *Mississippi as a Province, Territory, and State with Biographical Notices of Eminent Citizens* (Jackson: Power and Barksdale, 1880), has been quoted in several histories of the Creek War era. While the accuracy of the alleged transcript is highly suspect and refuted by most modern historians who have researched the topic, there is general agreement among scholars of the era that his message contained an implied, if not overt, call for a rejection of American culture, return to ancestral ways, and military preparedness.

CHAPTER TWO

1. For an overview of Creek attacks in the spring of 1812 and their consequences, see Waselkov, *Conquering Spirit*, 72–106; H. S. Halbert and T. H. Ball, *The Creek War of 1813 and 1814* (Chicago: Donohue and Henneberry, 1895), 105–19; Hudson, *Creek Paths and Federal Roads*, 97–102; Frank L. Owsley Jr., *Struggle for the Gulf Borderlands: The Creek War and the Battle of New Orleans, 1812–1815* (Tuscaloosa: University of Alabama Press, 1981), 15–16, 24–26; Thomas S. Woodward,

Woodward's Reminiscences of the Creek, or Muscogee Indians, Contained in Letters to Friends in Georgia and Alabama (Montgomery: Barrett and Wimbush, 1859), 32–34, 84–85; Tom Kanon, "The Kidnapping of Martha Crawley and Settler-Indian Relations Prior to the War of 1812," *Tennessee Historical Quarterly* 64 (Spring 2005): 3–23; Griffith, *McIntosh and Weatherford*, 80–88. Over a dozen settler or military forts eventually stood in the Tensaw region. An insightful firsthand perspective of the fear and reactions among Tensaw area settlers is found in Margaret Ervin Austill, "The Life of Margaret Ervin Austill," *Alabama Historical Quarterly* 6 (Spring 1944): 92–98.

2. James P. Kaetz, "Battle of Burnt Corn Creek," *Encyclopedia of Alabama*, http://www.encyclopediaofalabama.org/article/h-3081 (accessed September 2, 2016); Owsley, *Struggle for the Gulf Borderlands*, 30–33; Waselkov, *Conquering Spirit*, 98–102; Elizabeth Howard West, "A Prelude to the Creek War of 1813–14," *Florida Historical Quarterly* 18 (April 1940): 247–66; Stiggins, *Creek Indian History*, 98–103; Halbert and Ball, *Creek War*, 125–42; Albert James Pickett, *History of Alabama and Incidentally of Georgia and Mississippi from the Earliest Period* (Montgomery: River City Publishing, 2003), 521–57; Woodward, *Woodward's Reminiscences*, 84–85; Mike Bunn and Clay Williams, *Battle for the Southern Frontier: The Creek War and the War of 1812* (Charleston, SC: History Press, 2008), 31–33.

3. Waselkov's *A Conquering Spirit*, 116–38, contains the most detailed of the many studies of the Battle of Fort Mims yet published. Incorporating the great majority of known primary and secondary sources, the book is also informed by the author's archaeological investigation of the site. Waselkov's analysis forms the basis for the summary of the battle presented here. See also Waselkov, "Fort Mims Battle and Massacre," *Encyclopedia of Alabama*, http://www.encyclopediaofalabama.org/article/h-1121 (accessed September 2, 2016).

4. Waselkov, *Conquering Spirit*, 116–38. The next day after the affair at Fort Mims, Red Sticks massacred an entire family near a settler stockade in the vicinity known as Fort Sinquefield. A pitched battle took place there on September 2, 1813. See Mike Bunn, "Fort Sinquefield," *Encyclopedia of Alabama*, http://www.encyclopediaofalabama.org/article/h-3749 (accessed September 2, 2016); Howard T. Weir III, *A Paradise of Blood: The Creek War of 1813–14* (Yardley, PA: Westholme, 2016), 187–93; Halbert and Ball, *Creek War*, 177–89; Bunn and Williams, *Battle for the Southern Frontier*, 35–38.

5. Halbert and Ball, *Creek War*, 116, 122, 296–300; Claiborne, *Mississippi as a Province, Territory and State*, 336–37, 356; Owsley, *Struggle for the Gulf Borderlands*, 43–46.

6. "Notes furnished by Col. Jeremiah Austill in relation to the Canoe Fight and other engagements in which he was concerned in the memorable years 1813–1814," Pickett Papers, Alabama Department of Archives and History; Bunn and Williams, *Battle for the Southern Frontier*, 42.

7. Owsley, *Struggle for the Gulf Borderlands*, 47–48; Waselkov, *Conquering Spirit*, 164–66; Griffith, *McIntosh and Weatherford*, 126–32; Halbert and Ball, *Creek War*, 241–65; Pickett, *History of Alabama*, 574–77; Stiggins, *Creek Indian History*, 116–21; Dunbar Rowland, "Military History of Mississippi, 1803–1898," in *The Official Statistical Register of the State of Mississippi, 1908* (Jackson: Mississippi Department of Archives and History, 1908), 399; General Ferdinand Claiborne to Secretary of War John Armstrong, January 1, 1814, in John Brannan, *Official Letters of the Military and Naval Officers of the United States, during the War with Great Britain in the Years 1812, 13, 14, and 15* (Washington, DC: Way and Gideon, 1823). Weir, *Paradise of Blood*, 380–391; Bunn and Williams, *Battle for the Southern Frontier*, 43–46.

8. Weir, *Paradise of Blood*, 235–43, 255–61; Owsley, *Struggle for the Gulf Borderlands*, 51–54; Sean Michael O'Brien, *In Bitterness and in Tears: Andrew Jackson's Destruction of the Creeks and Seminoles* (Guilford, CT: Lyons Press, 2003), 93–96.

9. Peter A. Brannon, "Fort Mitchell References," *Alabama Historical Quarterly* 21 (1959): 1–13; Owsley, *Struggle for the Gulf Borderlands*, 54–59; Griffith, *McIntosh and Weatherford*, 124–26,

135–37; O'Brien, *In Bitterness and Tears*, 69–100, 125–27; Gordon Burns Smith, *History of the Georgia Militia, 1783–1861* (Milledgeville, GA: Boyd Publishing, 2000), 129–30; Stiggins, *Creek Indian History*, 124–33; Pickett, *History of Alabama*, 557–59, 584–86; George Cary Eggleston, *Red Eagle and the Wars with the Creek Indians* (New York: Dodd, Mead, 1878), 207–13; Peter A. Brannon, ed., "Journal of James Tait for the Year 1813," *Alabama Historical Quarterly* 2 (Winter 1940): 431–40; General John Floyd to General Pinckney, January 27, 1814, in Brannan, *Official Letters*, 283–85, 296–97; Bunn and Williams, *Battle for the Southern Frontier*, 59–63.

10. Willie Blount to Jackson, September 24, 1813, in John Spencer Bassett, ed., *Correspondence of Andrew Jackson*, vol. 1 (Washington, DC: Carnegie Institution, 1926), 320–21; Robert Remini, *Andrew Jackson: The Course of American Empire, 1767–1821* (New York: Harper and Row, 1977), 191.

11. Robert Remini, *Andrew Jackson and His Indian Wars* (New York: Viking, 2001), 62–66; Weir, *Paradise of Blood*, 214–29; Remini, *Andrew Jackson: Course of American Empire*, 194–97; O'Brien, *In Bitterness and Tears*, 73–74, 76–79; Davy Crockett, *Life of Davy Crockett* (New York: n.p., 1854), 75; Jackson to Blount, November 4, 1813, in Bassett, *Correspondence*, 34; Jackson to Willie Blount, November 15, 1813, in Bassett, *Correspondence*, 348–50. Talladega's aftermath did lead to one of the war's more regrettable episodes. A communication failure led to other Tennessee troops attacking and burning several Red Stick villages that had pledged to surrender following Talladega. Claiming to have been betrayed by Jackson, these particular Red Sticks vowed to fight to the death and were among the last to finally make peace. Owsley, *Struggle for the Gulf Borderlands*, 66–67; Weir, *Paradise of Blood*, 229–34; Bunn and Williams, *Battle for the Southern Frontier*, 75–76.

12. Remini, *Andrew Jackson: Course of American Empire*, 197–208; Weir, *Paradise of Blood*, 335–79; Jackson to Mrs. Jackson, January 28, 1813, in Bassett, *Correspondence*, 444–47; Owsley, *Struggle for the Gulf Borderlands*, 72–78; O'Brien, *In Bitterness and Tears*, 117–24; Bunn and Williams, *Battle for the Southern Frontier*, 80–81.

13. Tom Kanon, "'A Slow, Laborious Slaughter': The Battle of Horseshoe Bend," *Tennessee Historical Quarterly* 58 (Spring 1999): 2–15; Weir, *Paradise of Blood*, 391–428; James W. Holland, *Victory at the Horseshoe: Andrew Jackson and the Creek War* (Tuscaloosa: University of Alabama Press, 2004), 20–27; Ove Jensen, "Horseshoe Bend: A Living Memorial," in *Tohopeka: Rethinking the Creek War and the War of 1812* (Tuscaloosa: University of Alabama Press, 2012), 146–57; Remini, *Andrew Jackson: Course of American Empire*, 213–16; O'Brien, *In Bitterness and Tears*, 146–47; H. W. Brands, *Andrew Jackson: His Life and Times* (New York: Doubleday, 2005), 216–17; Jackson to Blount, March 31, 1814, in Bassett, *Correspondence*, 489–92; Jackson to Mrs. Jackson, April 1, 1814, in Bassett, *Correspondence*, 492–94; Jackson to Pinckney, March 31, 1814, in Bassett, *Correspondence*, 488–89; Bunn and Williams, *Battle for the Southern Frontier*, 81–84.

14. Remini, *Andrew Jackson and His Indian Wars*, 80–81; Remini, *Andrew Jackson: Course of American Empire*, 218–21; O'Brien, *In Bitterness and Tears*, 156–58; Pickett, *History of Alabama*, 593–95; Eggleston, *Red Eagle*, 329–39; John Reid and John Henry Eaton, *The Life of Andrew Jackson, Major General in the Service of the United States, Comprising a History of the War in the South from the Commencement of the Creek Campaign to the Termination of Hostilities before New Orleans* (Philadelphia: M. Carey and Son, 1817), 166–67.

15. Remini, *Andrew Jackson: Course of American Empire*, 221–22, 224–32; Reid and Eaton, *Life of Andrew Jackson*, 190–91; Owsley, *Struggle for the Gulf Borderlands*, 86–94; Weir, *Paradise of Blood*, 454–64; O'Brien, *In Bitterness and Tears*, 163. The full text of the Treaty of Fort Jackson can be found in Charles J. Kappler, ed., *Indian Treaties, 1778–1883* (New York: Interland, 1972), 107–10.

16. Owsley, *Struggle for the Gulf Borderlands*, 95–99, 101–2, 105, 109–12; Frank L. Owsley Jr., "British and Indian Activities in Spanish West Florida during the War of 1812," *Florida Historical*

Quarterly 46 (October 1967): 111–23; Remini, *Andrew Jackson: Course of American Empire*, 232–36; Robin Reilly, *The British at the Gates: The New Orleans Campaign in the War of 1812* (New York: G. P. Putnam's Sons, 1974), 172; Samuel Carter III, *Blaze of Glory: The Fight for New Orleans, 1814–1815* (New York: St. Martin's Press, 1971), 40–41.

17. Remini, *Andrew Jackson: Course of American Empire*, 239–41; Jackson to Manrique, August 6, 1814, in Bassett, *Correspondence*, 92–93; Jackson to Monroe, November 14, 1814, in Bassett, *Correspondence*, 96–99; Owsley, *Struggle for the Gulf Borderlands*, 112–19. For accounts of the Battle of New Orleans, see Robert Remini, *The Battle of New Orleans: Andrew Jackson and America's First Military Victory* (New York: Penguin, 1999); Arsène Lacarrière Latour, *Historical Memoir of the War in West Florida and Louisiana in 1814–1815* (New Orleans: Historic New Orleans Collection; Gainesville: University Press of Florida, 1999); Donald R. Hickey, *Glorious Victory: Andrew Jackson and the Battle of New Orleans* (Baltimore: Johns Hopkins University Press, 2015); Winston Groom, *Patriotic Fire: Andrew Jackson and Jean Laffite at the Battle of New Orleans* (New York: Vintage Books, 2006). For a detailed account of the second attempt by the British to reduce Fort Bowyer, see William S. Coker, *The Last Battle of the War of 1812: New Orleans, No, Fort Bowyer!* (Pensacola, FL: Perdido Bay Press, 1981); Bunn and Williams, *Battle for the Southern Frontier*, 97–115.

CHAPTER THREE

1. Quote taken from a description of the Alabama Territory, reprinted in the *Huntsville Republican*, October 7, 1817.

2. James Graham to Thomas Ruffin, November 9, 1817, in J. G. de Roulhac Hamilton, ed., *The Papers of Thomas Ruffin* (Raleigh, NC: Edwards and Broughton, 1918), 198.

3. Charles D. Lowery, "The Great Migration to the Mississippi Territory, 1798–1819," *Mississippi History Now*, November 2000, http://mshistorynow.mdah.state.ms.us/articles/169/the-great-migration-to-the-mississippi-territory-1798–1819 (accessed January, 2016); Charles D. Lowery, "The Great Migration to the Mississippi Territory, 1798–1819," *Journal of Mississippi History* 30 (August 1968): 173–92; Thomas P. Abernethy, *The South in the New Nation: 1789–1819* (Baton Rouge: Louisiana State University Press, 1961), 465; Edwin C. Bridges, *Alabama: The Making of an American State* (Tuscaloosa: University of Alabama Press, 2016), 57–60; Donna Cox Baker, "The Land Rush to Statehood: Alabama Fever," *Alabama Heritage* (Spring 2011): 36.

4. Lowery, "Great Migration," 182; Abernethy, *South in the New Nation*, 465–66; Pickett, *History of Alabama*, 466–69; Rogers et al., *Alabama: The History of a Deep South State*, 54–60; Jesse M. Wilkins, "Early Times in Wayne County," *Publications of the Mississippi Historical Society* 6 (1902): 265–72; Bradley G. Bond, ed., *Mississippi: A Documentary History* (Jackson: University Press of Mississippi, 2003), 43–45. For an overview of immigration to the Southwest during the era, see Clark and Guice, *Frontiers in Conflict:* Everett Dick, *The Dixie Frontier: A Social History* (New York: Knopf, 1948); Frank L. Owsley, "The Pattern of Migration and Settlement on the Southern Frontier," *Journal of Southern History* 11 (May 1945): 147–76; Joan E. Cashin, *A Family Venture: Men and Women on the Southern Frontier* (New York: Oxford University Press, 1991); James David Miller, *South by Southwest: Planter Emigration and Identity in the Slave South* (Charlottesville: University of Virginia Press, 2002); Ray Allen Billington and Martin Ridge, *Westward Expansion: A History of the American Frontier* (Albuquerque: University of New Mexico Press, 2001); Henry DeLeon Southerland Jr. and Jerry Elijah Brown, *The Federal Road through Georgia, the Creek Nation, and Alabama, 1806–1836* (Tuscaloosa: University of Alabama Press, 1989); Hudson, *Creek Paths and Federal Roads*; Harvey H. Jackson III, *Rivers of History: Life on the Coosa, Tallapoosa, Cahaba, and*

Alabama (Tuscaloosa: University of Alabama Press, 1995), 42–45; William C. Davis, *A Way through the Wilderness: The Natchez Trace and the Civilization of the Southern Frontier* (Baton Rouge: Louisiana State University Press, 1995), 82–103.

5. Davis, *A Way through the Wilderness*, 82–103.

6. Edward Chambers Betts, *Historic Huntsville, Alabama, 1804–1870* (Montgomery: Brown Printing, 1916), 6–7; Madison County Heritage Book Committee, *The Heritage of Madison County, Alabama* (Clanton, AL: Heritage Publishing Consultants, 1998), 261–66; David Byers, "A History of Early Settlement: Madison County before Statehood, 1808–1819," *Huntsville Historical Review*, special issue (2008): 42–59.

7. Byers, "History of Early Settlement," 42–59. Ironically, Hunt was forced to relocate when wealthy planter LeRoy Pope bought the tract of land he occupied at public auction in Nashville.

8. Austill, "Life of Margaret Ervin Austill," 92–98.

9. "Diary of Richard Breckinridge, 1816," in *Transactions of the Alabama Historical Society, 1898–1899*, ed. Thomas McAdory Owen (Tuscaloosa: Alabama Historical Society, 1904), 142–53.

10. Darrel E. Bigham, "From the Green Mountains to the Tombigbee: Henry Hitchcock in Territorial Alabama, 1817–1819," *Alabama Review* 26 (July 1973): 209–28; William H. Brantley Jr., "Henry Hitchcock of Mobile, 1816–1839," *Alabama Review* 5 (January 1952): 3–39; Herbert J. Lewis, "A Connecticut Yankee in Early Alabama: Henry Wilbourne Stevens and the Founding of Ordered Society, 1814–1823," *Alabama Review* 59 (April 2006): 83–106.

11. Gideon Lincecum, "Autobiography of Gideon Lincecum," *Publications of the Mississippi Historical Society* 8 (Oxford: Mississippi Historical Society, 1905): 443–519. See also Lois Wood Burkhalter, *Gideon Lincecum, 1793–1874: A Biography* (Austin: University of Texas Press, 1965).

12. Eugene L. Schwaab, ed., *Travels in the Old South, Selected from Periodicals of the Times* (Lexington: University Press of Kentucky, 1973), 202; Dupre, *Transforming the Cotton Frontier*, 100; Basil Hall, *Travels in North America, in the Years 1827 and 1828* (London: Simpkin and Marshall, 1830), 131–32; Bradley G. Bond, *Political Culture in the Nineteenth-Century South: Mississippi, 1830–1900* (Baton Rouge: Louisiana State University Press, 1995), 53–63; Lowery, "Great Migration," 188; Frank L. Owsley, *Plain Folk of the Old South* (Baton Rouge: Louisiana State University Press, 1949), 67–68, and "Pattern of Migration," 147–76; Dick, *Dixie Frontier*, 25.

13. Thomas P. Abernethy, *The Formative Period in Alabama, 1815–1828* (Tuscaloosa: University of Alabama Press, 1990), 30–43; Abernethy, *South in the New Nation*, 468–47; Clark and Guice, *Frontiers in Conflict*, 161–82; William B. Hamilton, "Mississippi in 1817: A Sociological and Economic Analysis," *Journal of Mississippi History* 34 (November 1967): 270–92; Lowery, "Great Migration"; John Solomon Otto, "The Migration of the Southern Plain Folk: An Interdisciplinary Synthesis," *Journal of Southern History* 51 (May 1985): 183–200; James P. Pate, ed., *The Reminiscences of George Strother Gaines, Pioneer Statesman of Early Alabama and Mississippi, 1805–1843* (Tuscaloosa: University of Alabama Press, 1998), 79. For a detailed account of the history of the Vine and Olive Company, see Rafe Blaufarb, *Bonapartists in the Borderlands: French Exiles and Refugees on the Gulf Coast, 1815–1835* (Tuscaloosa: University of Alabama Press, 2005), and Rafe Blaufarb, "Vine and Olive Company," *Encyclopedia of Alabama*, http://www.encyclopediaofalabama.org/article/h-1539 (accessed September 6, 2016); Eric Saugera, *Reborn in America: French Exiles and Refugees in the United States and the Vine and Olive Adventure, 1815–1865* (Tuscaloosa: University of Alabama Press, 2011).

14. Abernethy, *Formative Period*, 46–48; Alan V. Briceland, "Land, Law, and Politics on the Tombigbee Frontier, 1804," *Alabama Review* 33 (April 1980): 92–124; Haynes, *Mississippi Territory and the Southwest Frontier*, 33–34, 57–60; Clark and Guice, *Frontiers in Conflict*, 209; Abernethy, *Formative Period*, 57; James F. Foster, "Land Titles and Public Land Sales in Early Alabama," *Alabama Review* 16 (April 1963): 109–22; Dick, *Dixie Frontier*, 67–68; Frances C. Roberts, "Thomas Freeman—Surveyor of the Old Southwest," *Alabama Review* 40 (July 1987): 216–31; William J.

Morton, "Exploring The Mystery of Famed Surveyor Thomas Freeman: Just Who Was the Man Who Worked Alongside Famous U.S. Surveyor Andrew Ellicott?" *Point of Beginning*, http://www.pobonline.com/articles/97502-exploring-the-mystery-of-thomas-freeman (accessed February 4, 2016); "United States Land Offices in Alabama, 1803–1879," *Alabama Historical Quarterly* 17 (Fall 1955): 146–48; Griffith, *Alabama: A Documentary History*, 65.

15. James Benson Sellers, *Slavery in Alabama* (Tuscaloosa: University of Alabama Press, 1950), 147; Willis Brewer, *Alabama: Her History, Resources, War Record, and Public Men, from 1540 to 1872* (Montgomery: Barrett and Brown, 1872), 29–30, 44; Rogers et al., *Alabama: The History of a Deep South State*, 54; Abernethy, *Formative Period*, 72; Shawn A. Bivens, *Mobile, Alabama's People of Color: A Tricentennial History, 1702–2002* (Victoria, BC: Trafford, 2004), 41; see also David J. Libby, *Slavery and Frontier Mississippi, 1720–1835* (Jackson: University Press of Mississippi, 2004); Jim Barnett and Clark Burkett, "The Forks of the Road Slave Market at Natchez," *Journal of Mississippi History* 63 (Fall 2001): 169–88; Keith S. Hebert, "Slavery," *Encyclopedia of Alabama*, http://www.encyclopediaofalabama.org/article/h-2369 (accessed September 8, 2016).

16. The broad outlines of slavery in the antebellum South are chronicled in a host of outstanding studies focusing on the South at large and on individual states. Among the most useful for understanding the daily lives of slaves consulted for this study are Eugene D. Genovese, *Roll Jordan Roll: The World the Slaves Made* (New York: Random House, 1976); Elizabeth Fox-Genovese, *Within the Plantation Household: Black and White Women of the Old South* (Chapel Hill: University of North Carolina Press, 1988); John W. Blassingame, *The Slave Community: Plantation Life in the Antebellum South* (New York: Oxford University Press, 1979); Kenneth M. Stampp, *Peculiar Institution: Slavery in the Ante-bellum South* (New York: Random House, 1989); John Hebron Moore, *The Emergence of the Cotton Kingdom in the Old Southwest: Mississippi, 1770–1860* (Baton Rouge: Louisiana State Uniersity Press, 1988); Charles S. Sydnor, *Slavery in Mississippi* (Baton Rouge: Louisiana State University Press, 1966); Libby, *Slavery and Frontier Mississippi*; Sellers, *Slavery in Alabama*. Firsthand accounts of slave life a generation after the period under study can be found in Andrew Waters, ed., *Prayin' to Be Set Free: Personal Accounts of Slavery in Mississippi* (Winston-Salem, NC: John F. Blair, 2002), and the Federal Writers' Project, *Alabama Slave Narratives* (Bedford, MA: Applewood Books, 2006).

17. Federal Writers' Project, *Alabama Slave Narratives.*

18. Carter, ed., *TheTerritorial Papers*, 6: 299; Leah Atkins, "The First Legislative Session: The General Assembly of Alabama, Huntsville, 1819," *Alabama Review* 23 (January 1970): 39; Malcom Cook McMillan, "The Alabama Constitution of 1819: A Study of Constitution-Making on the Frontier," *Alabama Review* 3 (October 1950): 280; Malcolm Cook McMillan, *Constitutional Development in Alabama, 1798–1901: A Study in Politics, the Negro, and Sectionalism* (Spartanburg, SC: Reprint Company, 1978), 42; Herbert James Lewis, *Clearing the Thickets: A History of Antebellum Alabama* (New Orleans: Quid Pro Quo Books, 2013), 139, 155–56. The revolts mentioned are chronicled in dozens of books focusing on each event. For a summary of them and others that were significant in shaping the institution of slavery in America, see Eugene D. Genovese, *From Rebellion to Revolution: Afro-American Slave Revolts in the Making of the Modern World* (Baton Rouge: Louisiana State University Press, 1979).

19. Harriet E. Amos, *Cotton City: Urban Development in Antebellum Mobile* (Tuscaloosa: University of Alabama Press, 2001), 21; Charles S. Davis, *Cotton Kingdom in Alabama* (Philadelphia: Porcupine Press, 1974); Kenneth E. Phillips and Janet Roberts, "Cotton," *Encyclopedia of Alabama*, http://www.encyclopediaofalabama.org/article/h-1491 (accessed September 2016); Robert J. Vejnar, "Plantation Agriculture," *Encyclopedia of Alabama*, http://www.encyclopediaofalabama.org/article/h-1832 (accessed September 8, 2016); Libby, *Slavery and Frontier Mississippi*,

41–46; John Hebron Moore, *Agriculture in Ante-bellum Mississippi* (New York: Bookman, 1958), 30, 42–43; Abernethy, *Formative Period*, 80–82; Sellers, *Slavery in Alabama*, 69–71.

CHAPTER FOUR

1. Anne Newport Royall, *Letters from Alabama, on Various Subjects* (Washington, DC: Anne Royall, 1830), 54–58. For a description of the environment of the nineteenth-century South, see Jack Temple Kirby, *Mockingbird Song: Ecological Landscapes of the South* (Chapel Hill: University of North Carolina Press, 2006).

2. William Darby, *The Emigrants Guide to the Western and Southwestern States and Territories: Comprising a Geographical and Statistical Description of the States of Louisiana, Mississippi, Tennesseee, Kentucky, and Ohio* (New York: Kirk and Mercein, 1818), 121; John Hawkins Napier III, *Lower Pearl River's Piney Woods: Its Land and People* (University: University of Mississippi Center for the Study of Southern Culture, 1985), 53; Waselkov, *Conquering Spirit*, 122–23. For information on the "little ice age," see Brian Fagan, *The Little Ice Age: How Climate Made History, 1300–1850* (New York: Basic Books, 2000). For more on the eruption of Mount Tambora and its unusual climatic effects in 1816, see William Klingaman and Nicholas Klingaman, *The Year without Summer: 1816 and the Volcano That Darkened the World and Changed History* (New York: St. Martin's Press, 2013); Gillen D'Arcy Wood, *Tambora: The Eruption That Changed the World* (Princeton, NJ: Princeton University Press, 2014).

3. Mills Lane, *Architecture of the Old South: Mississippi and Alabama* (New York: Beehive Press, 1989), 12–15; E. Bryding Adams, ed., *Made in Alabama: A State Legacy* (Birmingham: Birmingham Museum of Art, 1995), 33–39; Rhoda Coleman Ellison, *Bibb County: The First Hundred Years, 1818–1918* (Tuscaloosa: University of Alabama Press, 1984), 17–18; Betts, *Historic Huntsville*, 8; Abernethy, *Formative Period*, 35–36; Weymouth T. Jordan, *Ante-bellum Alabama: Town and Country* (Tuscaloosa: University of Alabama Press, 1957), 24; Clark and Guice, *Frontiers in Conflict*, 195–96; Dick, *Dixie Frontier*, 27–30; Mary Ann Neely, *Old Alabama Town: An Illustrated Guide* (Tuscaloosa: University of Alabama Press, 2002), 30–31; Eugene M. Wilson, *Alabama Folk Houses* (Montgomery: Alabama Historical Commission, 1975).

4. Jordan, *Ante-bellum Alabama*, 67–82; Dick, *Dixie Frontier*, 98–99; Dupre, *Transforming the Cotton Frontier*, 20–21; see also Owsley, *Plain Folk*.

5. Owsley, *Plain Folk*, 23–90, and "Pattern of Migration,"149–51; Clark and Guice, *Frontiers in Conflict*, 99–116; Otto, "Migration of the Southern Plain Folk," 183; Lowery, "Great Migration," 187–88; Sam Bowers Hilliard, *Hog Meat and Hoecake: A Geographical View of Food Supply in the Heart of the Old South* (Madison: University of Wisconsin Press, 1966), 92–119; Moore, *Emergence of the Cotton Kingdom*, 146–47; Jack D. L. Holmes, "Livestock in Spanish Natchez," *Journal of Mississippi History* 23 (January 1961): 15–37; Richard S. Lackey, ed., *Frontier Claims in the Lower South* (Baton Rouge: Provincial Press, 1977), 21–54; Davis, *A Way through the Wilderness*, 66–67.

6. Rogers et al., *Alabama: The History of a Deep South State*, 58–59; Dick, *Dixie Frontier*, 287–92; Hilliard, *Hog Meat and Hoecake*, 37, 157; Moore, *Agriculture in Ante-bellum Mississippi*, 57–60; Marius M. Carriere Jr., "Mount Locust Plantation: The Development of Southwest Mississippi during the Frontier Period, 1810–1830," *Journal of Mississippi History* 48 (August 1986): 192; Christopher Morris, *Becoming Southern: The Evolution of a Way of Life, Warren County and Vicksburg, Mississippi, 1770–1860* (New York: Oxford University Press, 1995), 32; Dupre, *Transforming the Cotton Frontier*, 21; Abernethy, *Formative Period*, 164–65; Clark and Guice, *Frontiers in Conflict*, 196–98; Lewis, *Clearing the Thickets*, 176–77.

7. Owsley, *Plain Folk*, 106–26; Dick, *Dixie Frontier*, 98–99; Waldo W. Braden, *The Oral Tradition in the South* (Baton Rouge: Louisiana State University Press, 1983), 26–27; Virginia Van der Veer Hamilton, *Alabama: A History* (New York: W. W. Norton, 1984), 16; Davis, *A Way through the Wilderness*, 121–28; Rogers et al., *Alabama: The History of a Deep South State*, 60.

8. Jackson, *Rivers of History*, 45; Clark and Guice, *Frontiers in Conflict*, 183–206; Davis, *A Way through the Wilderness*, 82–130; G. Ward Hubbs, *Guarding Greensboro: A Confederate Company in the Making of a Southern Community* (Athens: University of Georgia Press, 2003), 16–17.

9. Carter, *Territorial Papers*, 5: 322–26.

10. In Bigham, "From the Green Mountains to the Tombigbee," 215; G. Ward Hubbs, *Tuscaloosa: Portrait of an Alabama County* (Northridge, CA: Windsor, 1987), 20–21.

11. *Huntsville Democrat*, October 14, 1823. Harvey H. Jackson III, *Inside Alabama: A Personal History of My State* (Tuscaloosa: University of Alabama Press, 2004), 27, 47–48; Rogers et al., *Alabama: The History of a Deep South State*, 67; Schwaab, *Travels in the Old South*, 197–202; Margaret Deschamps Moore, "Protestantism in the Mississippi Territory," *Journal of Mississippi History* 29 (November 1967): 358–70; Jordan, *Ante-bellum Alabama*, 23; James F. Doster, "Early Settlements on the Tombigbee and Tensaw Rivers," *Alabama Review* 12 (April 1959): 83–94; Herbert James Lewis, *Lost Capitals of Alabama* (Charleston, SC: History Press, 2014); 35–36; Wayne Flynt, *Alabama Baptists: Southern Baptists in the Heart of Dixie* (Tuscaloosa: University of Alabama Press, 1998), 4–7; Clark and Guice, *Frontiers in Conflict*, 190–93; Abernethy, *Formative Period*, 158–60; Davis, *A Way through the Wilderness*, 131–59.

12. J. Barry Vaughn, *Bishops, Bourbons, and Big Mules: A History of the Episcopal Church in Alabama* (Tuscaloosa: University of Alabama Press, 2013), 11–18; Charles E. Nolan, *A History of the Archdiocese of Mobile, Alabama* (Strasbourg, France: Éditions du Signe, 2012), 16–23. See also James William Marshall and Robert Strong, *The Presbyterian Church in Alabama: A Record of the Growth of the Presbyterian Church from Its Beginnings in 1811 in the Eastern Portion of the Mississippi Territory to the Centennial of the Synod of Alabama in 1936* (Montgomery: Presbyterian Historical Society of Alabama, 1977); Randy J. Sparks, *Religion in Mississippi* (Jackson: University Press of Mississippi, 2001).

13. Davis, *A Way through the Wilderness*, 104–30.

14. For the early history of Huntsville, see Lewis, *Lost Capitals*, 41–63; Betts, *Historic Huntsville*; Ranee G. Pruitt, ed., *Eden of the South: A Chronology of Huntsville, Alabama, 1805–2005* (Huntsville: Huntsville–Madison County Public Library, 2005). For the history of Florence and Coffee's role in its founding, see Sarah Lawless, "Florence," *Encyclopedia of Alabama*, http://www.encyclopediaofalabama.org/article/h-2121 (accessed October 5, 2016); Carolyn M. Barske, "Florence: Discovering Alabama's Renaissance City," *Alabama Heritage* (Winter 2015): 8–19; Gordon T. Chappell, "John Coffee: Surveyor and Land Agent," *Alabama Review* 14 (July 1963): 185–248, and "John Coffee: Land Speculator and Planter," *Alabama Review* 22 (January 1969): 24–43; Dupre, *Transforming the Cotton Frontier*, 45. For an overview of the early history of Tuscaloosa, see Hubbs, *Tuscaloosa: Portrait of an Alabama County*, and Thomas P. Clinton, "Early History of Tuscaloosa," *Alabama Historical Quarterly* 1 (Spring 1930): 169–74. For information on the founding era of Montgomery, see Wayne Flynt, *Montgomery: An Illustrated History* (Woodland Hills, CA: Windsor, 1980); Clanton W. Williams, *The Early History of Montgomery and Incidentally of the State of Alabama* (Tuscaloosa: University of Alabama Press, 1976). For a history of early Selma, see Alston Fitts III, *Selma: Queen City of the Black Belt* (Selma: Clairmont Press, 1989). For information on Cahawba, see Lewis, *Lost Capitals*, 65–97, and Herbert J. Lewis, "Cahaba," *Encyclopedia of Alabama*, http://www.encyclopediaofalabama.org/article/h-1543 (accessed October 2, 2016); Todd Keith, *Old Cahawba* (Brierfield, AL: Cahaba Trace Commission, 2003). For information on the founding of Centreville and Chotard's efforts, see Ellison, *Bibb County*, 1–40, and Bibb County

Heritage Book Committee, *Heritage of Bibb County, Alabama* (Clanton, AL: Heritage Publishing Consultants, 1998).

15. For an overview of the early history of Mobile, see Michael V. Thomason, ed., *Mobile: The New History of Alabama's First City* (Tuscaloosa: University of Alabama Press, 2001); Melton McLaurin and Michael Thomason, *Mobile: The Life and Times of a Great Southern City* (Woodland Hills, CA: Windsor Publications, 1981); Amos, *Cotton City*. Information on the city's creole population taken from Virginia Meacham Gould, "The Free Creoles of Color of the Antebellum Gulf Ports of Mobile and Pensacola: A Struggle for the Middle Ground," in *Creoles of Color in the Gulf South*, ed. James H. Dormon (Knoxville: University of Tennessee Press, 1996), 28–50; Bivens, *Mobile, Alabama's People of Color*, 42. A brief history of Blakeley can be found in Grant D. Hiatt, "Blakeley," *Encyclopedia of Alabama*, http://www.encyclopediaofalabama.org/article/h-3023 (accessed October 3, 2016); James C. Parker, "Blakeley: A Frontier Seaport," *Alabama Review* 27 (January 1974): 39–51; W. Stuart Harris, *Dead Towns of Alabama* (Tuscaloosa: University of Alabama Press, 1977), 63–64. For a summary description of yellow fever and its impact on the region in the time period, see Margaret Humphreys, *Yellow Fever and the South* (Baltimore: Johns Hopkins University Press, 1999). Commonly known at the time as "yellow jack," the fever is a viral disease spread by mosquitoes. It usually struck early Alabama communities in the late summer or early fall. After a short incubation period it manifests itself in a variety of unpleasant ways, including fever, headache, nausea, muscle pains, and the telltale yellowish tint to the skin caused by liver damage. Many of those who contracted the dread illness died within a matter of days—sometimes even hours.

16. Daniel Savage Gray, "Frontier Journalism: Newspapers in Antebellum Alabama," *Alabama Historical Quarterly* 37 (Fall 1975): 183–91; F. Wilbur Helmbold, "Early Alabama Newspapermen, 1810–1820," *Alabama Review* 12 (January 1959): 53–65; Douglas C. McMurtrie, "A Note on Joseph P. Forster, Pioneer Alabama Printer," *Alabama Historical Quarterly* 5 (Summer 1943): 234–36; Abernethy, *Formative Period*, 152–55; Adams, *Made in Alabama*, 141, 143, 283–84, 298, 302.

17. Jack K. Williams, "Crime and Punishment in Alabama, 1819–1840," *Alabama Review* 6 (January 1953): 21–22; Amos, *Cotton City*, 16; John Sledge, *The Mobile River* (Columbia: University of South Carolina Press, 2015), 86, 252; John S. Sledge and Sheila Hagler, *The Pillared City: Greek Revival Mobile* (Athens: University of Georgia Press, 2009), 26–27.

CHAPTER FIVE

1. Carter, *Territorial Papers*, 5: 290, 297–98, 6: 3, 36–39, 253–57, 337, 339, 347; Richard A. McLemore, "The Division of the Mississippi Territory," *Journal of Mississippi History* 5 (1943): 79–80; Claiborne, *Mississippi as a Province, Territory, and State*, 297; Laura D. S. Harrell, "Imprints toward Statehood," *Journal of Mississippi History* 29 (November 1967): 429–42; Abernethy, *Formative Period*, 45; Thomas Hart Benton, ed. *Abridgement of the Debates of Congress, from 1789 to 1856*, vol. 4 (New York, D. Appleton, 1857), 411; Riley, "Location of the Boundaries of Mississippi," 173–74; Haynes, *Mississippi Territory and the Southwest Frontier*, 336.

2. Haynes, "Road to Statehood," in *A History of Mississippi*, vol. 1, ed. Richard A. McLemore (Jackson: University and College Press of Mississippi, 1973), 219–20; Riley, "Location of the Boundaries," 175.

3. Carter, *Territorial Papers*, 6: 708–17, 748–49, 763–64; Richard McLemore and Nannie McLemore, "The Birth of Mississippi," *Journal of Mississippi History* 39 (November 1967): 260; Claiborne, *Mississippi as a Province, Territory, and State*, 299; McLemore, "Division of the Mississippi Territory," 80; Haynes, "Formation of the Territory," 244–45; Riley, "Location of the

Boundaries," 170–73, 176–81; Haynes, *Mississippi Territory and the Southwest Frontier*, 341–42; Clark and Guice, *Frontiers in Conflict*, 217–18; Abernethy, *Formative Period*, 49–50; *A Century of Lawmaking for a New Nation: U.S. Congressional Documents and Debates, 1774–1875: Statutes at Large*, 14th Congress, 2nd Session, http://memory.loc.gov/cgi-bin/ampage?collId=llsl&fileName=003/llsl003.db&recNum=412 (accessed October 9, 2016), 348–49; "An Act to Establish a Separate Territorial Government for the Eastern Part of the Mississippi Territory," 371–73, 15th Congress, 1st Session, http://memory.loc.gov/cgi-bin/ampage?collId=llsl&fileName=003/llsl003.db&recNum=513 (accessed October 9, 2016), "Resolution for the State of Mississippi into the Union," 472–43.

4. Daniel S. Dupre, "William Wyatt Bibb," *Encyclopedia of Alabama*, http://www.encyclopediaofalabama.org/article/h-1416 (accessed October 11, 2016); Samuel L. Webb and Margaret E. Armbrester, eds., *Alabama Governors: A Political History of the State* (Tuscaloosa: University of Alabama Press, 2001), 13–17; J. Mills Thornton, "Broad River Group," *Encyclopedia of Alabama*, http://www.encyclopediaofalabama.org/article/h-1137 (accessed October 11, 2016); Thornton, *Politics and Power in a Slave Society*, 7–20; Ruth Ketring Nuermberger, "The 'Royal Party' in Early Alabama Politics," *Alabama Review* 6 (April 1953): 83–95, and (July 1953): 200–212; Lewis, *Clearing the Thickets*, 114, 147–48. For more on the "Era of Good Feelings," see George Dangerfield, *The Era of Good Feelings* (New York: Harcourt Brace Jovanovich, 1952), and Daniel Walker Howe, *What Hath God Wrought: The Transformation of America, 1815–1848* (New York: Oxford University Press, 2007).

5. William H. Brantley, *Three Capitals: A Book about the First Three Capitals of Alabama* (Tuscaloosa: University of Alabama Press, 1976), 24–25, 28; "An Act to Establish a Separate Territorial Government for the Eastern Part of the Mississippi Territory," Statutes at Large, 14th Congress, 2nd Session, 371–73; http://memory.loc.gov/cgi-bin/ampage?collId=llsl&fileName=003/llsl003.db&recNum=412 (accessed January 3, 2016); Abernethy, *Formative Period*, 50; Lewis, *Lost Capitals of Alabama*, 28; Lewis, *Clearing the Thickets*, 116–20; Malcolm Cook McMillan, *Constitutional Development in Alabama, 1798–1901: A Study in Politics, the Negro, and Sectionalism* (Spartanburg, SC: Reprint Company, 1978), 25.

6. Thornton, *Politics and Power*, 7; Betts, *Historic Huntsville*, 34; Historical Census Browser, retrieved October 9, 2016, from the University of Virginia, Geospatial and Statistical Data Center, http://mapserver.lib.virginia.edu/collections/.

7. Brantley, *Three Capitals*, 26–27, 32–34; Herbert J. Lewis, "Cahaba," *Encyclopedia of Alabama*, http://www.encyclopediaofalabama.org/article/h-1543 (accessed October 5, 2016); Lewis, *Clearing the Thickets*, 120–21; Lewis, *Lost Capitals*, 37; Webb and Armbrester, *Alabama Governors*, 12; Carter, *Territorial Papers*, 18: 794–95; John Scott, "Cahaba: Hallowed Ground," *Alabama Heritage* (Winter 2011): 12–23; Nan Fairley, "The Lost Capitals of St. Stephens and Cahawba," *Alabama Heritage* (Spring 1998): 23; McMillan, *Constitutional Development in Alabama*, 25, 37; McMillan, "Alabama Constitution of 1819," 272–73; Rogers et al., *Alabama: The History of a Deep South State*, 66.

8. Royall, *Letters from Alabama*, 130. The impact of Indian land cessions on the amount of territory in Alabama open for American settlement is most graphically demonstrated by comparing maps produced before and after these treaties. Among the most authoritative in circulation prior to 1815 is Francis Shallus's "Mississippi Territory" (Philadelphia: Published by Matthew Carey and Son, 1814), http:alabamamaps.ua.edu (accessed October 9, 2016). The map shows the widely scattered American settlements and most of what became Alabama still in native hands. Perhaps the best of the few maps produced of the Alabama Territory is John Melish's "Map of Alabama Constructed from the Surveys in the General Land Office and Other Documents" (Philadelphia: Published by John Melish, 1820), retrieved from the Library of Congress, https://www.loc.gov/item/2012590211 (accessed March 6, 2016). For an overview of each tribe's cessions of land during the period, see Hahn, "Creeks in Alabama"; Greg O'Brien, "Chickasaws in Alabama,"

Encyclopedia of Alabama, http://www.encyclopediaofalabama.org/article/h-1487 (accessed October 9, 2016); Greg O'Brien, "Choctaws in Alabama," http://www.encyclopediaofalabama.org/article/h-1186 (accessed October 9, 2016); Susan M. Abram, "Cherokees in Alabama," *Encyclopedia of Alabama*, http://www.encyclopediaofalabama.org/article/h-1186 (accessed October 9, 2016).

9. Information on Creek diplomacy in the colonial era taken from Braund, *Deerskins and Duffels*; Ethridge, *Creek Country*; Saunt, *A New Order of Things: Property, Power, and the Transformation of the Creek Indians, 1733–1816*. See also O'Brien, "Chickasaws in Alabama"; O'Brien, "Choctaws in Alabama"; Hahn, "Creeks in Alabama"; Abram, "Cherokees in Alabama." Dawson A. Phelps, "Colbert Ferry and Selected Documents," *Alabama Historical Quarterly* 25 (Fall and Winter 1963): 203–26; Dawson A. Phelps, "The Natchez Trace in Alabama," *Alabama Review* 7 (January 1954): 28–37; Charles W. Watts, "Colbert's Reserve and the Chickasaw Treaty of 1818," *Alabama Review* 7 (October 1959): 272–80; Susan M. Abram, "Sequoyah," *Encyclopedia of Alabama*, http://www.encyclopediaofalabama.org/article/h-2159 (accessed October 20, 2016). There are numerous biographies of Sequoyah in print, but among the most compelling accounts of his life in relation to the creation of the syllabary is found in chapter one of Ellen Cushman, *The Cherokee Syallabary: Writing the People's Perseverance* (Norman: University of Oklahoma Press, 2011).

10. Pate, *The Reminiscences of George Strother Gaines*, 40–42; Robert P. Collins, "A Swiss Traveler in the Creek Nation: The Diary of Lukas Vischer, March, 1824," *Alabama Review* 59 (October 2006): 243–84.

11. The Reverend Charles Edward Crenshaw, "Indian Massacres in Butler County in 1818," in *Transactions of the Alabama Historical Society, 1899–1903*, ed. Thomas McAdory Owen (Montgomery: Alabama Historical Society, 1904), 99–101; Pickett, *History of Alabama*, 619–22; William H. Jenkins, "Alabama Forts, 1700–1838," *Alabama Review* 12 (July 1959): 179; Carter, *Territorial Papers of the United States*, 18: 304, 318, 331–33.

12. Carter, *Territorial Papers of the United States*, 18: 459–61; *Acts of the Fifteenth Congress of the United States*, "An Act to Enable the People of Alabama Territory to Form a Constitution and State Government, for Admission of Such State into the Union, on an Equal Footing with the Original States," Statutes at Large, 15th Congress, 2nd Session, 489–92, http://memory.loc.gov/cgi-bin/ampage?collId=llsl&fileName=003/llsl003.db&recNum=530 (accessed January 5, 2016); Thomas McAdory Owen, ed., "The Visit of President James Monroe to Alabama Territory, June 1, 1819," in *Transactions of the Alabama Historical Society, 1898–1899* (Tuscaloosa: Alabama Historical Society, 1899), 154–58; Lewis, *Lost Capitals of Alabama*, 50.

13. *Journal of the Convention of the Alabama Territory* (Huntsville: John Boardman, 1819); Lewis, *Lost Capitals*, 50; Betts, *Historic Huntsville*, 35; McMillan, "Alabama Constitution of 1819: A Study of Constitution-Making on the Frontier," 263–86; McMillan, *Constitutional Development in Alabama*, 30; Lewis, *Clearing the Thickets*, 133–36; Abernethy, *Formative Period*, 53–54; Rogers et al., *Alabama: The History of a Deep South State*, 68.

14. *Journal of the Convention of the Alabama Territory*; Jackson, *Inside Alabama*, 52; McMillan, *Constitutional Development in Alabama*, 46; McMillan, "Alabama Constitution of 1819," 270; Clark and Guice, *Frontiers in Conflict*, 229; Lewis, *Clearing the Thickets*, 136–41.

CHAPTER SIX

1. Lewis, *Clearing the Thickets*, 144–46; Dupre, "William Wyatt Bibb."

2. Atkins, "The First Legislative Session," 31–43; Lewis, *Clearing the Thickets*, 144–46, 150–59; Adrian G. Daniel, "Navigational Development of Muscle Shoals, 1807–1890," *Alabama Review* 14 (October 1961): 252–54; Amos, *Cotton City*, 20; Abernethy, *Formative Period*, 98; Daniel Fate

Brooks, "William Rufus King," *Encyclopedia of Alabama*, http://www.encyclopediaofalabama.org/article/h-1886 (accessed October 10, 2016); Hugh C. Bailey, "John Williams Walker," *Encyclopedia of Alabama,* http://www.encyclopediaofalabama.org/article/h-1181 (accessed October 11, 2016).

3. "Resolution Declaring the Admission of the State of Alabama Into the Union," Statutes at Large, 16th Congress, 1st Session, 608; http://memory.loc.gov/cgi-bin/ampage?collId=llsl&fileName=003/llsl003.db&recNum=649 (accessed January 5, 2016), Brantley, *Three Capitals*, 59.

4. Michael Ward, "The Panic of 1819," *Encyclopedia of Alabama*, http://www.encyclopediaofalabama.org/article/h-2568 (accessed February 22, 2016).

5. Dupre, *Transforming the Cotton Frontier*, 6–10; 50–60; Webb and Armbrester, *Alabama Governors*, 16; Lewis, *Clearing the Thickets*, 143. For more on early Alabama's financial institutions and the effect of the downturn on both them and the territorial and state economy, see William H. Brantley, *Banking in Alabama, 1816–1860* (Birmingham: Oxmoor Press, 1961).

6. Dupre, *Transforming the Cotton Frontier*, 37, 104–5; Thornton, *Politics and Power in a Slave Society*, 7–14; Thornton, "Broad River Group"; Bridges, *Alabama*, 64–66; Lewis, *Lost Capitals of Alabama*, 42–43; Betts, *Historic Huntsville*, 23–25; Abernethy, *Formative Period*, 50, 137; Webb and Armbrester, *Alabama Governors*, 16–17.

7. Dupre, *Transforming the Cotton Frontier*, 75, 80–81; Brantley, *Banking in Alabama*, 16–18; Lewis, *Clearing the Thickets*, 162–63, 169; Nuermberger, "The 'Royal Party' in Early Alabama Politics," 88–95, 211–12; Ward, "The Panic of 1819" (accessed February 22, 2016); Webb and Armbrester, *Alabama Governors*, 16–18; Dupre, "William Wyatt Bibb"; Dupre, "Thomas Bibb," *Encyclopedia of Alabama*, http://www.encyclopediaofalabama.org/article/h-1531 (accessed October 12, 2016); Ellison, *Bibb County*, 1.

8. Scott, "Cahaba: Hallowed Ground," 12–23; Griffith, *Alabama: A Documentary History*, 225; Lewis, "Cahaba"; Lewis, *Lost Capitals*, 65–85; Keith, *Old Cahawba*; Brantley, *Three Capitals*, 60–64.

9. Dupre, "Thomas Bibb"; Daniel S. Dupre, "Israel Pickens," *Encyclopedia of Alabama*, http://www.encyclopediaofalabama.org/article/h-1912 (accessed October 12, 2016).

10. Hugh C. Bailey, "Israel Pickens, People's Politician," *Alabama Review* 17 (April 1964): 83–100; Dupre, "Israel Pickens"; Webb and Armbrester, *Alabama Governors*, 17–20; Abernethy, *Formative Period*, 114–18; Jackson, *Inside Alabama*, 55–57.

11. Jackson, *Inside Alabama*, 55–57; Brantley, *Banking in Alabama*; Rogers et al., *Alabama: The History of a Deep South State*, 79; Lewis, *Clearing the Thickets*, 171–73; Thomas M. Owen, "The Genesis of the University of Alabama," *Alabama Historical Quarterly* 2 (Summer 1940): 169–88; Hugh C. Bailey, "John Murphy," *Encyclopedia of Alabama*, http://www.encyclopediaofalabama.org/article/h-1466 (accessed October 12, 2016).

12. Thornton, *Politics and Power in a Slave State*, 20–24; Webb and Armbrester, *Alabama Governors*, 20–45; Abernethy, *Formative Period*, 120–51; Lewis, *Clearing the Thickets*, 177; Jackson, *Inside Alabama*, 72; Frederick M. Beatty, "Whig Party," *Encyclopedia of Alabama*, http://www.encyclopediaofalabama.org/article/h-1173 (accessed October 13, 2016). For an overview of Jackson's influence in the political culture of the era, see Edward Pessen, *Jacksonian America: Society, Personality, and Politics* (Urbana: University of Illinois Press, 1978).

13. Willis Brewer, *Alabama: Her History, Resources, War Record, and Public Men* (Spartanburg, SC: Reprint Company, 1975), 45; Rufus Ward, *The Tombigbee River Steamboats: Rollodores, Dead Heads, and Side-Wheelers* (Charleston, SC: History Press, 2010), 23; James C. Parker, "Blakeley: A Frontier Seaport," *Alabama Review* 27 (January 1974): 43; Weymouth T. Jordan, "Antebellum Mobile: Alabama's Agricultural Emporium," *Alabama Review* 1 (July 1948): 185; Jackson, *Rivers of History*, 47; Abernethy, *Formative Period*, 95–96; Jack N. Nelms, "Early Days with the Alabama River Steamboats," *Alabama Review* 37 (January 1984): 13–23; Robert O. Mellown, "Steamboats

in Alabama," *Encyclopedia of Alabama*, http://www.encyclopediaofalabama.org/article/h-1803 (accessed October 13, 2016).

14. Information on Lafayette's visit taken from "General Lafayette's Visit to Alabama in 1825," *Alabama Historical Quarterly* 14 (1952): 66–75; Tennant S. McWilliams, "The Marquis and the Myth: Lafayette's Visit to Alabama, 1825," *Alabama Review* 22 (April 1969): 135–45; Lucile Cary Lowry, "Lafayette's Visit to Georgia and Alabama," *Alabama Historical Quarterly* 8 (Spring 1946): 35–40; Herbert J. Lewis, "Lafayette's Visit to Alabama," *Encyclopedia of Alabama*, http://www.encyclopediaofalabama.org/article/h-2152 (accessed October 13, 2016); Edwin C. Bridges, "'The Nation's Guest': The Marquis de Lafayette's Tour of Alabama," *Alabama Heritage* 102 (Fall 2011): 8–17; Rogers et al., *Alabama: The History of a Deep South State*, 81; Jackson, *Inside Alabama*, 58–60; McLaurin and Thomason, *Mobile: The Life and Times of a Great Southern City*, 39; Jackson, *Rivers of History*, 55–58; "Lafayette's Visit to Claiborne," *Alabama Historical Quarterly* 19 (Summer 1957): 259–78;. Woodward, *Woodward's Reminiscences*; Auguste Levasseur, *Lafayette in America in 1824 and 1825*, vol. 2 (Philadelphia: Carey and Lea, 1829).

15. Woodward, *Woodward's Reminiscences*, 66–70; Levasseur, *Lafayette in America*, 76–77.

16. "General Lafayette's Visit to Alabama in 1825," 67–68; McWilliams, "The Marquis and the Myth: Lafayette's Visit to Alabama, 1825," 142–45; Lowry, "Lafayette's Visit to Georgia and Alabama," 38–39; Jackson, *Inside Alabama*, 59; Jackson, *Rivers of History*, 56–57; "Lafayette's Visit to Claiborne," 264; McLaurin and Thomason, *Mobile: The Life and Times of a Great Southern City*, 39; Levasseur, *Lafayette in America*, 84.

17. Abernethy, *Formative Period*, 137; Jackson, *Inside Alabama*, 61; Jackson, *Rivers of History*, 57; Lewis, *Clearing the Thickets*, 188–90; Lewis, *Lost Capitals of Alabama*, 84–85; Brantley, *Three Capitals*, 46–47; Scott, "Cahaba: Hallowed Ground"; Keith, *Old Cahawba*; Rogers et al., *Alabama: The History of a Deep South State*, 76, 82.

18. Lewis, *Clearing the Thickets*, 188; Rogers et al., *Alabama: The History of a Deep South State*, 82.

19. Lewis, *Lost Capitals of Alabama*, 99–108; Hubbs, *Tuscaloosa: Portrait of an Alabama County*, 19–21; William H. Ely, "Elyton, Alabama, and the Connecticut Asylum: The Letters of William H. Ely, 1820–1821," ed. William S. Hoole, *Alabama Review* 3 (January 1950): 36–39; Thomas P. Clinton, "Early History of Tuscaloosa," *Alabama Historical Quarterly* 1 (Spring 1930): 169–74.

20. Lewis, *Lost Capitals of Alabama*, 108–9.

EPILOGUE

1. Historical Census Browser, retrieved October 14, 2016, from the University of Virginia, Geospatial and Statistical Data Center, http://mapserver.lib.virginia.edu/collections/.

2. Pickett, *History of Alabama*, 669.

BIBLIOGRAPHY

BOOKS

Abernethy, Thomas P. *The Formative Period in Alabama, 1815–1828*. Tuscaloosa: University of Alabama Press, 1990.

———. *The South in the New Nation, 1789–1819*. Baton Rouge: Louisiana State University Press, 1961.

Adams, E. Bryding, ed., *Made in Alabama: A State Legacy*. Birmingham: Birmingham Museum of Art, 1995.

Amos, Harriet E. *Cotton City: Urban Development in Antebellum Mobile*. Tuscaloosa: University of Alabama Press, 2001.

Barnett, James F., Jr. *Mississippi's American Indians*. Jackson: University Press of Mississippi, 2012.

Bassett, John Spencer, ed. *Correspondence of Andrew Jackson*. Vol. 1. Washington, DC: Carnegie Institution, 1926.

Bemis, Samuel Flagg. *Pinckney's Treaty: America's Advantage from Europe's Distress, 1783–1800*. New Haven, CT: Yale University Press, 1960.

Benton, Thomas Hart, ed. *Abridgement of the Debates of Congress, from 1789 to 1856*. Vol. 4. New York: D. Appleton, 1857.

Betts, Edward Chambers. *Early History of Huntsville, Alabama, 1804–1870*. Montgomery: Brown Printing, 1916.

Bibb County Heritage Book Committee. *Heritage of Bibb County, Alabama*. Clanton, AL: Heritage Publishing Consultants, 1998.

Billington, Ray Allen, and Martin Ridge. *Westward Expansion: A History of the American Frontier*. Albuquerque: University of New Mexico Press, 2001.

Bivens, Shawn A. *Mobile, Alabama's People of Color: A Tricentennial History, 1702–2002*. Victoria, BC: Trafford, 2004.

Blassingame, John W. *The Slave Community: Plantation Life in the Antebellum South*. New York: Oxford University Press, 1979.

Blaufarb, Rafe. *Bonapartists in the Borderlands: French Exiles and Refugees on the Gulf Coast, 1815–1835*. Tuscaloosa: University of Alabama Press, 2005.

Bond, Bradley G., ed. *Mississippi: A Documentary History*. Jackson: University Press of Mississippi, 2003.

———. *Political Culture in the Nineteenth-Century South: Mississippi, 1830–1900*. Baton Rouge: Louisiana State University Press, 1995.

Braden, Waldo W. *The Oral Tradition in the South*. Baton Rouge: Louisiana State University Press, 1983.

Brands, H. W. *Andrew Jackson: His Life and Times*. New York: Doubleday, 2005.

Brannan, John. *Official Letters of the Military and Naval Officers of the United States, during the War with Great Britain in the Years 1812, 13, 14, and 15*. Washington, DC: Way and Gideon, 1823.

Brantley, William H. *Banking in Alabama, 1816–1860*. Birmingham: Oxmoor Press, 1961.

———. *Three Capitals: A Book about the First Three Capitals of Alabama*. Tuscaloosa: University of Alabama Press, 1976.

Braund, Kathryn E. Holland. *Deerskins and Duffels: The Creek Indian Trade with Anglo-America, 1685–1815*. Lincoln: University of Nebraska Press, 1993.

Brewer, Willis. *Alabama: Her History, Resources, War Record, and Public Men, from 1540 to 1872*. Montgomery: Barrett and Brown, 1872.

Bridges, Edwin C. *Alabama: The Making of an American State*. Tuscaloosa: University of Alabama Press, 2016.

Brown, Lynda W., Donald B. Dodd, Lloyd H. Cornett Jr., and Alma D. Steading. *Alabama History: An Annotated Bibliography*. Westport, CT: Greenwood Press, 1998.

Bunn, Mike, and Clay Williams. *Battle for the Southern Frontier: The Creek War and the War of 1812*. Charleston, SC: History Press, 2008.

Burkhalter, Lois Wood. *Gideon Lincecum, 1793–1874: A Biography*. Austin: University of Texas Press, 1965.

Busbee, Westley F., Jr. *Mississippi: A History*. Wheeling, IL: Harland Davidson, 2005.

Carter, Clarence, ed. *The Territorial Papers of the United States*. Washington, DC: Government Printing Office, 1937–38.

Carter, Samuel, III. *Blaze of Glory: The Fight for New Orleans, 1814–1815*. New York: St. Martin's Press, 1971.

Cashin, Joan E. *A Family Venture: Men and Women on the Southern Frontier*. New York: Oxford University Press, 1991.

A Century of Lawmaking for a New Nation: U.S. Congressional Documents and Debates, 1774–1875, Statutes at Large. http://memory.loc.gov/ammem/amlaw/lawhome.html.

Christopher, Raven, and Gregory A. Waselkov. *Archaeological Survey of the Old Federal Road in Alabama*. Montgomery: Alabama Department of Transportation, 2012.

Claiborne, J. F. H. *Mississippi as a Province, Territory, and State with Biographical Notices of Eminent Citizens*. Jackson: Power and Barksdale, 1880.

Clark, Thomas D., and John W. Guice. *Frontiers in Conflict: The Old Southwest, 1795–1830*. Norman: University of Oklahoma Press, 1989.

Coker, William S. *The Last Battle of the War of 1812: New Orleans, No, Fort Bowyer!* Pensacola, FL: Perdido Bay Press, 1981.

Crockett, Davy. *Life of Davy Crockett*. New York: n.p., 1854.

Cushman, Ellen. *The Cherokee Syllabary: Writing the People's Perseverance*. Norman: University of Oklahoma Press, 2011.

Dangerfield, George. *The Era of Good Feelings*. New York: Harcourt Brace Jovanovich, 1952.

Darby, William. *The Emigrants Guide to the Western and Southwestern States and Territories: Comprising a Geographical and Statistical Description of the States of Louisiana, Mississippi, Tennessee, Kentucky, and Ohio*. New York: Kirk and Mercein, 1818.

Davis, Charles S. *Cotton Kingdom in Alabama*. Philadelphia: Porcupine Press, 1974.

Davis, William C. *The Rogue Republic: How Would-Be Patriots Waged the Shortest Revolution in American History*. New York: Houghton Mifflin Harcourt, 2011.

———. *A Way through the Wilderness: The Natchez Trace and the Civilization of the Southern Frontier*. Baton Rouge: Louisiana State University Press, 1995.

Dick, Everett. *The Dixie Frontier: A Social History*. New York: Knopf, 1948.

Drake, Benjamin. *Life of Tecumseh, and His Brother the Prophet: With a Historical Sketch of the Shawnee Indians*. Cincinnati: E. Morgan, 1841.

Dupre, Daniel S. *Transforming the Cotton Frontier: Madison County, Alabama, 1800–1840*. Baton Rouge: Louisiana State University Press, 1997.

Eggleston, George Cary. *Red Eagle and the Wars with the Creek Indians*. New York: Dodd, Mead, 1878.

Ellison, Rhoda Coleman. *Bibb County: The First Hundred Years, 1818–1918*. Tuscaloosa: University of Alabama Press, 1984.

Ethridge, Robbie. *Creek Country: The Creek Indians and Their World*. Chapel Hill: University of North Carolina Press, 2003.

Fagan, Brian. *The Little Ice Age: How Climate Made History, 1300–1850*. New York: Basic Books, 2000.

Federal Writers' Project. *Alabama Slave Narratives*. Bedford, MA: Applewood Books, 2006.

Fitts, Alston, III. *Selma: Queen City of the Black Belt*. Selma: Clairmont Press, 1989.

Flynt, Wayne. *Alabama Baptists: Southern Baptists in the Heart of Dixie*. Tuscaloosa: University of Alabama Press, 1998.

———. *Montgomery: An Illustrated History*. Woodland Hills, CA: Windsor, 1980.

Foster, Thomas. *The Collected Works of Benjamin Hawkins, 1796–1810*. Tuscaloosa: University of Alabama Press, 2003.

Fox-Genovese, Elizabeth. *Within the Plantation Household: Black and White Women of the Old South*. Chapel Hill: University of North Carolina Press, 1988.

Gamble, Robert. *The Alabama Catalog: A Guide to the Early Architecture of the State*. Tuscaloosa: University of Alabama Press, 1987.

Genovese, Eugene D. *From Rebellion to Revolution: Afro-American Slave Revolts in the Making of the Modern World*. Baton Rouge: Louisiana State University Press, 1979.

———. *Roll Jordan Roll: The World the Slaves Made*. New York: Random House, 1976.

Grant, C. L. *Letters, Journals, and Writings of Benjamin Hawkins*. Savannah, GA: Beehive Press, 1980.

Green, Michael D. *The Politics of Indian Removal: Creek Government and Society in Crisis*. Lincoln: University of Nebraska Press, 1982.

Griffith, Lucille. *Alabama: A Documentary History to 1900*. Tuscaloosa: University of Alabama Press, 1987.

Griffith, Benjamin, Jr. *McIntosh and Weatherford: Creek Indian Leaders*. Tuscaloosa: University of Alabama Press, 1988.

Groom, Winston. *Patriotic Fire: Andrew Jackson and Jean Laffite at the Battle of New Orleans*. New York: Vintage Books, 2006.

Hahn, Steven C. *The Invention of the Creek Nation, 1670–1763*. Lincoln: University of Nebraska Press, 2004.

Halbert, H. S., and T. H. Ball. *The Creek War of 1813 and 1814*. Chicago: Donohue and Henneberry, 1895.

Hale, Jennifer. *Historic Plantations of Alabama's Black Belt*. Charleston, SC: History Press, 2009.

Hall, Basil. *Travels in North America, in the Years 1827 and 1828*. London: Simpkin and Marshall, 1830.

Hamilton, J. G. de Roulhac, ed. *The Papers of Thomas Ruffin*. Raleigh, NC: Edwards and Broughton, 1918.

Hamilton, Peter J. *Colonial Mobile: An Historical Study Largely from Original Sources, of the Alabama-Tombigbee Basin and the Old South West.* Boston: Houghton Mifflin, 1910.

Hamilton, Virginia Van der Veer. *Alabama: A History.* New York: W. W. Norton, 1984.

Harris, W. Stuart. *Dead Towns of Alabama.* Tuscaloosa: University of Alabama Press, 1977.

Haynes, Robert V. *The Mississippi Territory and the Southwest Frontier, 1795–1817.* Lexington: University Press of Kentucky, 2010.

———. *The Natchez District and the American Revolution.* Jackson: University Press of Mississippi, 1976.

Henri, Florette. *The Southern Indians and Benjamin Hawkins.* Norman: University of Oklahoma Press, 1986.

Hickey, Donald R. *Glorious Victory: Andrew Jackson and the Battle of New Orleans.* Baltimore: Johns Hopkins University Press, 2015.

Higginbotham, Jay. *Old Mobile: Fort Louis de la Louisiane, 1702–1711.* Mobile: Museum of the City of Mobile, 1977.

Hilliard, Sam Bowers. *Hog Meat and Hoecake: A Geographical View of Food Supply in the Heart of the Old South.* Madison: University of Wisconsin Press, 1966.

Holland, James W. *Victory at the Horseshoe: Andrew Jackson and the Creek War.* Tuscaloosa: University of Alabama Press, 2004.

Holmes, Jack D. L. *Honor and Fidelity: The Louisiana Infantry Regiment and the Louisiana Militia Companies, 1766–1821.* Birmingham: n.p., 1965.

Howe, Daniel Walker. *What Hath God Wrought: The Transformation of America, 1815–1848.* New York: Oxford University Press, 2007.

Hubbs, G. Ward. *Guarding Greensboro: A Confederate Company in the Making of Southern Community.* Athens: University of Georgia Press, 2003.

———. *Tuscaloosa: Portrait of an Alabama County.* Northridge, CA: Windsor, 1987.

Hudson, Angela Pulley. *Creek Paths and Federal Roads: Indians, Settlers, and Slaves and the Making of the American South.* Chapel Hill: University of North Carolina Press, 2010.

Humphreys, Margaret. *Yellow Fever and the South.* Baltimore: Johns Hopkins University Press, 1999.

Jackson, Harvey H., III. *Inside Alabama: A Personal History of My State.* Tuscaloosa: University of Alabama Press, 2004.

———. *Rivers of History: Life on the Coosa, Tallapoosa, Cahaba, and Alabama.* Tuscaloosa: University of Alabama Press, 1995.

James, D. Clayton. *Antebellum Natchez.* Baton Rouge: Louisiana State University Press, 1968.

Jordan, Weymouth T. *Ante-bellum Alabama: Town and Country.* Tuscaloosa: University of Alabama Press, 1957.

Journal of the Convention of the Alabama Territory. Huntsville: John Boardman, 1819.

Kappler, Charles J., ed. *Indian Treaties, 1778–1883.* New York: Interland, 1972.

Keith, Todd. *Old Cahawba.* Brierfield, AL: Cahaba Trace Commission, 2003.

Kirby, Jack Temple. *Mockingbird Song: Ecological Landscapes of the South.* Chapel Hill: University of North Carolina Press, 2006.

Klingaman, William, and Nicholas Klingaman. *The Year without Summer: 1816 and the Volcano That Darkened the World and Changed History.* New York: St. Martin's Press, 2013.

Lackey, Richard S., ed. *Frontier Claims in the Lower South.* Baton Rouge: Provincial Press, 1977.

Lane, Mills. *Architecture of the Old South: Mississippi and Alabama.* New York: Beehive Press, 1989.

Latour, Arsène Lacarrière. *Historical Memoir of the War in West Florida and Louisiana in 1814–1815.* New Orleans: Historic New Orleans Collection; Gainesville: University Press of Florida, 1999.

Levasseur, Auguste. *Lafayette in America in 1824 and 1825.* Vol. 2. Philadelphia: Carey and Lea, 1829.

Lewis, Herbert James. *Clearing the Thickets: A History of Antebellum Alabama*. New Orleans: Quid Pro Quo Books, 2013.

———. *Lost Capitals of Alabama*. Charleston, SC: History Press, 2014.

Libby, David J. *Slavery and Frontier Mississippi, 1720–1835*. Jackson: University Press of Mississippi, 2004.

Madison County Heritage Book Committee. *The Heritage of Madison County, Alabama*. Clanton, AL: Heritage Publishing Consultants, 1998.

Marshall, James William, and Robert Strong. *The Presbyterian Church in Alabama: A Record of the Growth of the Presbyterian Church from Its Beginnings in 1811 in the Eastern Portion of the Mississippi Territory to the Centennial of the Synod of Alabama in 1936*. Montgomery: Presbyterian Historical Society of Alabama, 1977.

McLaurin, Melton, and Michael Thomason. *Mobile: The Life and Times of a Great Southern City*. Woodland Hills, CA: Windsor Publications, 1981.

McMillan, Malcolm Cook. *Constitutional Development in Alabama, 1798–1901: A Study in Politics, the Negro, and Sectionalism*. Spartanburg, SC: Reprint Company, 1978.

Miller, James David. *South by Southwest: Planter Emigration and Identity in the Slave South*. Charlottesville: University of Virginia Press, 2002.

Montulé, Édouard de. *A Voyage to North America and the West Indies in 1817*. London: Sir Richard Phillips and Company, 1821.

Moore, Edith W. *Natchez under-the-Hill*. Natchez: Southern Historical Publications, 1958.

Moore, John Hebron. *Agriculture in Ante-bellum Mississippi*. New York: Bookman, 1958.

———. *The Emergence of the Cotton Kingdom in the Old Southwest: Mississippi, 1770–1860*. Baton Rouge: Louisiana State University Press, 1988.

Morris, Christopher. *Becoming Southern: The Evolution of a Way of Life, Warren County and Vicksburg, Mississippi, 1770–1860*. New York: Oxford University Press, 1995.

Napier, John Hawkins, III. *Lower Pearl River's Piney Woods: Its Land and People*. University: University of Mississippi Center for the Study of Southern Culture, 1985.

Neely, Mary Ann. *Old Alabama Town: An Illustrated Guide*. Tuscaloosa: University of Alabama Press, 2002.

Nolan, Charles E. *A History of the Archdiocese of Mobile, Alabama*. Strasbourg, France: Éditions du Signe, 2012.

O'Brien, Sean Michael. *In Bitterness and In Tears: Andrew Jackson's Destruction of the Creeks and Seminoles*. Guilford, CT: Lyons Press, 2003.

Owsley, Frank L. *Plain Folk of the Old South*. Baton Rouge: Louisiana State University Press, 1949.

Owsley, Frank L., Jr. *Struggle for the Gulf Borderlands: The Creek War and the Battle of New Orleans, 1812–1815*. Tuscaloosa: University of Alabama Press, 1981.

Pate, James P., ed. *The Reminiscences of George Strother Gaines, Pioneer Statesman of Early Alabama and Mississippi, 1805–1843*. Tuscaloosa: University of Alabama Press, 1998.

Pessen, Edward. *Jacksonian America: Society, Personality, and Politics*. Urbana: University of Illinois Press, 1978.

Pickett, Albert James. *History of Alabama and Incidentally of Georgia and Mississippi from the Earliest Period*. Montgomery: River City Publishing, 2003.

Polk, Noel, ed. *Natchez before 1830*. Jackson: University Press of Mississippi, 1989.

Pound, Merrit B. *Benjamin Hawkins, Indian Agent*. Athens: University of Georgia Press, 1951.

Pruitt, Paul McWhorter, Jr. *Taming Alabama: Lawyers and Reformers, 1804–1929*. Tuscaloosa: University of Alabama Press, 2010.

Pruitt, Ranee G., ed. *Eden of the South: A Chronology of Huntsville, Alabama, 1805–2005*. Huntsville: Huntsville–Madison County Public Library, 2005.

Reid, John, and John Henry Eaton. *The Life of Andrew Jackson, Major General in the Service of the United States, Comprising a History of the War in the South from the Commencement of the Creek Campaign to the Termination of Hostilities before New Orleans*. Philadelphia: M. Carey and Son, 1817.

Reilly, Robin. *The British at the Gates: The New Orleans Campaign in the War of 1812*. New York: G. P. Putnam's Sons, 1974.

Remini, Robert. *Andrew Jackson and His Indian Wars*. New York: Viking, 2001.

———. *Andrew Jackson: The Course of American Empire, 1767–1821*. New York: Harper and Row, 1977.

———. *The Battle of New Orleans: Andrew Jackson and America's First Military Victory*. New York: Penguin, 1999.

Rodriguez, Junius P., ed. *The Louisiana Purchase: A Historical and Geographical Encyclopedia*. Santa Barbara, CA: ABC-Clio, 2002.

Rogers, William Warren, Robert David Ward, Leah Rawls Atkins, and Wayne Flynt. *Alabama: The History of a Deep South State*. Tuscaloosa: University of Alabama Press, 1994.

Rowe, Stephen M. *From a Love of History: The A. S. Williams III Americana Collection at the University of Alabama*. Tuscaloosa: University of Alabama Press, 2013.

Royall, Anne Newport. *Letters from Alabama, on Various Subjects*. Washington, DC: Anne Royall, 1830.

Saugera, Eric. *Reborn in America: French Exiles and Refugees in the United States and the Vine and Olive Adventure, 1815–1865*. Tuscaloosa: University of Alabama Press, 2011.

Saunt, Claudio. *A New Order of Things: Property, Power, and the Transformation of the Creek Indians, 1733–1816*. New York: Cambridge University Press, 1999.

Schwaab, Eugene L., ed. *Travels in the Old South, Selected from Periodicals of the Times*. Lexington: University Press of Kentucky, 1973.

Sellers, James Benson. *Slavery in Alabama*. Tuscaloosa: University of Alabama Press, 1950.

Sledge, John S. *The Mobile River*. Columbia: University of South Carolina Press, 2015.

Sledge, John S., and Sheila Hagler. *The Pillared City: Greek Revival Mobile*. Athens: University of Georgia Press, 2009.

Smith, Gordon Burns. *History of the Georgia Militia, 1783–1861*. Milledgeville, GA: Boyd Publishing, 2000.

Southerland, Henry deLeon, Jr., and Jerry Elijah Brown. *The Federal Road through Georgia, the Creek Nation, and Alabama, 1806–1836*. Tuscaloosa: University of Alabama Press, 1989.

Sparks, Randy J. *Religion in Mississippi*. Jackson: University Press of Mississippi, 2001.

Stampp, Kenneth M. *Peculiar Institution: Slavery in the Ante-bellum South*. New York: Random House, 1989.

Stewart, David O. *American Emperor: Aaron Burr's Challenge to Jeffersonian America*. New York: Simon and Schuster, 2011.

Stiggins, George. *Creek Indian History*. Birmingham: Birmingham Public Library Press, 1989.

Sugden, John. *Tecumseh: A Life*. New York: Henry Holt, 1997.

Sydnor, Charles S. *Slavery in Mississippi*. Baton Rouge: Louisiana State University Press, 1966.

Thomason, Michael V., ed. *Mobile: The New History of Alabama's First City*. Tuscaloosa: University of Alabama Press, 2001.

Thornton, J. Mills. *Politics and Power in a Slave Society: Alabama, 1800–1860*. Baton Rouge: Louisiana State University Press, 1978.

Vaughn, J. Barry. *Bishops, Bourbons, and Big Mules: A History of the Episcopal Church in Alabama*. Tuscaloosa: University of Alabama Press, 2013.

Ward, Rufus. *The Tombigbee River Steamboats: Rollodores, Dead Heads, and Side-Wheelers.* Charleston, SC: History Press, 2010.

Waselkov, Gregory A. *A Conquering Spirit: Fort Mims and the Redstick War of 1813–1814.* Tuscaloosa: University of Alabama Press, 2006.

Waters, Andrew, ed. *Prayin' to Be Set Free: Personal Accounts of Slavery in Mississippi.* Winston-Salem, NC: John F. Blair, 2002.

Webb, Samuel L., and Margaret E. Armbrester, eds. *Alabama Governors: A Political History of the State.* Tuscaloosa: University of Alabama Press, 2001.

Weir, Howard T., III. *A Paradise of Blood: The Creek War of 1813–14.* Yardley, PA: Westholme, 2016.

Williams, Clanton W. *The Early History of Montgomery and Incidentally of the State of Alabama.* Tuscaloosa: University of Alabama Press, 1976.

Wilson, Eugene M. *Alabama Folk Houses.* Montgomery: Alabama Historical Commission, 1975.

Wood, Gillen D'Arcy. *Tambora: The Eruption That Changed the World.* Princeton, NJ: Princeton University Press, 2014.

Woodward, Thomas S. *Woodward's Reminiscences of the Creek, or Muscogee Indians, Contained in Letters to Friends in Georgia and Alabama.* Montgomery: Barrett and Wimbush, 1859.

ARTICLES

Abram, Susan M. "Cherokees in Alabama." *Encyclopedia of Alabama*, http://www.encyclopediaofalabama.org/article/h-1186.

———. "Sequoyah." *Encyclopedia of Alabama*, http://www.encyclopediaofalabama.org/article/h-2159.

Atkins, Leah. "The First Legislative Session: The General Assembly of Alabama, Huntsville, 1819." *Alabama Review* 23 (January 1970): 30–44.

Austill, Margaret Ervin. "Life of Margaret Ervin Austill." *Alabama Historical Quarterly* 6 (Spring 1944): 92–98.

Baker, Donna Cox. "The Land Rush to Statehood: Alabama Fever." *Alabama Heritage* (Spring 2011): 35–43.

Bailey, Hugh C. "Israel Pickens, People's Politician." *Alabama Review* 17 (April 1964): 83–100.

———. "John Murphy." *Encyclopedia of Alabama*, http://www.encyclopediaofalabama.org/article/h-1466.

———. "John Williams Walker." *Encyclopedia of Alabama*, http://www.encyclopediaofalabama.org/article/h-1181.

Barnett, Jim, and Clark Burkett. "The Forks of the Road Slave Market at Natchez." *Journal of Mississippi History* 63 (Fall 2001): 169–88.

Barske, Carolyn M. "Florence: Discovering Alabama's Renaissance City." *Alabama Heritage* (Winter 2015): 8–19.

Beatty, Frederick M. "Whig Party." *Encyclopedia of Alabama*, http://www.encyclopediaofalabama.org/article/h-1173.

Bigham, Darrel E. "From the Green Mountains to the Tombigbee: Henry Hitchcock in Territorial Alabama, 1817–1819." *Alabama Review* 26 (July 1973): 209–28.

Blaufarb, Rafe. "Vine and Olive Colony." *Encyclopedia of Alabama*, http://www.encyclopediaofalabama.org/article/h-1539.

Blevins, Brooks. "Cattle Raising in Antebellum Alabama." *Alabama Review* 51 (October 1998): 266–91.

Brannon, Peter A. "Fort Mitchell References." *Alabama Historical Quarterly* 21 (1959): 1–13.

———. ed. "Journal of James Tait for the Year 1813." *Alabama Historical Quarterly* 2 (Winter 1940): 431–40.

Brantley, William H., Jr. "Henry Hitchcock of Mobile, 1816–1839." *Alabama Review* 5 (January 1952): 3–39.

Breckinridge, Richard. "Diary of Richard Breckinridge, 1816." In *Transactions of the Alabama Historical Society, 1898–1899*, edited by Thomas McAdory Owen, 142–53. Tuscaloosa: Alabama Historical Society, 1904.

Briceland, Alan V. "Ephraim Kirby: Mr. Jefferson's Emissary on the Tombigbee-Mobile Frontier in 1804." *Alabama Review* 24 (April 1971): 83–113.

———. "Land, Law, and Politics on the Tombigbee Frontier, 1804." *Alabama Review* 33 (April 1980): 92–124.

Bridges, Edwin C. "'The Nation's Guest': The Marquis de Lafayette's Tour of Alabama." *Alabama Heritage* 102 (Fall 2011): 8–17.

Brooks, Daniel Fate. "Fort Sinquefield." *Encyclopedia of Alabama*, http://www.encyclopediaofalabama.org/article/h-3749.

———. "Spanish West Florida." *Encyclopedia of Alabama*, http://www.encyclopediaofalabama.org/article/h-3748.

———. "William Rufus King." *Encyclopedia of Alabama*, http://www.encyclopediaofalabama.org/article/h-1886.

Bunn, Mike. "Fort Sinquefield." *Encyclopedia of Alabama*, http://www.encyclopediaofalabama.org/article/h-3749.

———. "Spanish West Florida." *Encyclopedia of Alabama*, http://www.encyclopediaofalabama.org/article/h-3748.

Byers, David. "A History of Early Settlement: Madison County before Statehood, 1808–1819." *Huntsville Historical Review*. Special issue (2008): 42–59.

Carriere, Marius M., Jr. "Mount Locust Plantation: The Development of Southwest Mississippi during the Frontier Period, 1810–1830." *Journal of Mississippi History* 48 (August 1986): 187–98.

Chambers, Nella J. "The Creek Indian Factory at Fort Mitchell." *Alabama Historical Quarterly* 21 (1959): 15–53.

Chappell, Gordon T. "John Coffee: Land Speculator and Planter." *Alabama Review* 22 (January 1969): 24–43.

———. "John Coffee: Surveyor and Land Agent." *Alabama Review* 14 (July 1963): 185–248.

Clinton, Thomas P. "Early History of Tuscaloosa." *Alabama Historical Quarterly* 1 (Spring 1930): 169–74.

Cobbs, Hamner. "Geography of the Vine and Olive Colony." *Alabama Review* 14 (April 1961): 83–97.

Collins, Robert P. "A Swiss Traveler in the Creek Nation: The Diary of Lukas Vischer, March, 1824." *Alabama Review* 59 (October 2006): 243–84.

Crenshaw, Charles Edward. "Indian Massacres in Butler County in 1818." In *Transactions of the Alabama Historical Society, 1899–1903*, edited by Thomas McAdory Owen, 99–102. Tuscaloosa: Alabama Historical Society, 1904

Daniel, Adrian G. "Navigational Development of Muscle Shoals, 1807–1890." *Alabama Review* 14 (October 1961): 251–58.

Doss, Chriss. "Early Settlement of Bearmeat Cabin Frontier." *Alabama Review* 22 (October 1969): 270–83.

Doss, Harriet E. Amos. "The Rise and Fall of an Alabama Founding Father, Gabriel Moore." *Alabama Review* 53 (July 2000): 163–76.

Doster, James F. "Early Settlements on the Tombigbee and Tensaw Rivers." *Alabama Review* 12 (April 1959): 83–94.

———. "Land Titles and Public Land Sales in Early Alabama." *Alabama Review* 16 (April 1963): 108–24.

Dupre, Daniel S. "Israel Pickens." *Encyclopedia of Alabama*, http://www.encyclopediaofalabama.org/article/h-1912.

———. "Thomas Bibb," *Encyclopedia of Alabama*, http://www.encyclopediaofalabama.org/article/h-1531.

———. "William Wyatt Bibb." *Encyclopedia of Alabama*, http://www.encyclopediaofalabama.org/article/h-1416.

Ely, William H. "Elyton, Alabama, and the Connecticut Asylum: The Letters of William H. Ely, 1820–1821." Edited by William S. Hoole. *Alabama Review* 3 (January 1950): 36–39.

Emerson, E. O. "The Bonapartist Exiles in Alabama." *Alabama Review* 11 (April 1958): 135–43.

"Establishment of the Alabama Territory." *Alabama Historical Quarterly* 24 (Spring 1962): 97–128.

Fairley, Nan. "The Lost Capitals of St. Stephens and Cahawba." *Alabama Heritage* (Spring 1998): 18–31.

Foster, James F. "Land Titles and Public Land Sales in Early Alabama." *Alabama Review* 16 (April 1963): 109–22.

Gallalee, Jack C. "Andrew Ellicott and the Ellicott Stone." *Alabama Review* 18 (April 1965): 92–105.

"General Lafayette's Visit to Alabama in 1825." *Alabama Historical Quarterly* 14 (1952): 66–75.

Gould, Virginia Meacham. "The Free Creoles of Color of the Antebellum Gulf Ports of Mobile and Pensacola: A Struggle for the Middle Ground." In *Creoles of Color in the Gulf South*, edited by James H. Dormon, 28–50. Knoxville: University of Tennessee Press, 1996.

Gray, Daniel Savage. "Frontier Journalism: Newspapers in Antebellum Alabama." *Alabama Historical Quarterly* 37 (Fall 1975): 183–91.

Haarmann, Albert. "The Spanish Conquest of British West Florida, 1779–1781." *Florida Historical Quarterly* 39 (October 1960): 107–34.

Hahn, Steven C. "Creeks in Alabama." *Encyclopedia of Alabama*, http://www.encyclopediaofalabama.org/article/h-1088.

Hamilton, William B. "Mississippi in 1817: A Sociological and Economic Analysis." *Journal of Mississippi History* 34 (November 1967): 270–92.

Harrell, Laura D. S. "Imprints toward Statehood." *Journal of Mississippi History* 29 (November 1967): 429–42.

Haynes, Robert V. "Early Washington County, Alabama." *Alabama Review* 18 (July 1965): 183–200.

———. "The Formation of the Territory." In *A History of Mississippi*, vol. 1, edited by Richard A. McLemore, 174–216. Jackson: University and College Press of Mississippi, 1973.

———. "The Road to Statehood." In *A History of Mississippi*, vol. 1, edited by Richard A. McLemore, 217–50. Jackson: University and College Press of Mississippi, 1973.

Hebert, Keith S. "Slavery." *Encyclopedia of Alabama*, http://www.encyclopediaofalabama.org/article/h-2369.

Helmbold, F. Wilbur. "Early Alabama Newspapermen, 1810–1820." *Alabama Review* 12 (January 1959): 53–65.

Hiatt, Grant D. "Blakeley." *Encyclopedia of Alabama*, http://www.encyclopediaofalabama.org/article/h-3023.

Holmes, Jack D. L. "Alabama's Forgotten Settlers: Notes on the Spanish Mobile District, 1780–1813." *Alabama Historical Quarterly* 33 (Summer 1971): 87–97.

———. "Livestock in Spanish Natchez." *Journal of Mississippi History* 23 (January 1961): 15–37.

———. "Mobile's Great Hurricane of 1819." *Alabama Historical Quarterly* 43 (Winter 1981): 322–32.

———. "A Spanish Province, 1779–1798." In *History of Mississippi*, vol. 1, edited by Richard A. McLemore, 158–73. Jackson: University and College Press of Mississippi, 1973.

Irons, George Vernon. "River Ferries in Alabama before 1861." *Alabama Review* 4 (January 1951): 22–37.

Jenkins, William H. "Alabama Forts, 1700–1838." *Alabama Review* 12 (July 1959): 163–79.

Jensen, Ove. "Horseshoe Bend: A Living Memorial." In *Tohopeka: Rethinking the Creek War and the War of 1812*, 146–57. Tuscaloosa: University of Alabama Press, 2012.

Jones, Virginia K., ed. "The Bowie Letters, 1819 and 1821." *Alabama Historical Quarterly* 22 (Winter 1960): 231–43.

Jordan, Weymouth T. "Antebellum Mobile: Alabama's Agricultural Emporium." *Alabama Review* 1 (July 1948): 180–202.

Kaetz, James P. "Battle of Burnt Corn Creek." *Encyclopedia of Alabama*, http://www.encyclopediaofalabama.org/article/h-3081.

Kanon, Tom. "The Kidnapping of Martha Crawley and Settler-Indian Relations Prior to the War of 1812." *Tennessee Historical Quarterly* 64 (Spring 2005): 3–23.

———. "'A Slow, Laborious Slaughter': The Battle of Horseshoe Bend." *Tennessee Historical Quarterly* 58 (Spring 1999): 2–15.

"Lafayette's Visit to Claiborne." *Alabama Historical Quarterly* 19 (Summer 1957): 259–78.

Lamplugh, George R. "Yazoo Land Fraud." *New Georgia Encyclopedia*, http://www.georgiaencyclopedia.org/articles/history-archaeology/yazoo-land-fraud.

Lawless, Sarah. "Florence." *Encyclopedia of Alabama*, http://www.encyclopediaofalabama.org/article/h-2121.

Lengel, Leland L. "The Road to Fort Mims: Judge Harry Toulmin's Observations on the Creek War, 1811–1813." *Alabama Review* 29 (January 1976): 16–36.

Lewis, Herbert J. "Cahaba." *Encyclopedia of Alabama*, http://www.encyclopediaofalabama.org/article/h-1543.

———. "A Connecticut Yankee in Early Alabama: Henry Wilbourne Stevens and the Founding of Ordered Society, 1814–1823." *Alabama Review* 59 (April 2006): 83–106.

———. "Lafayette's Visit to Alabama." *Encyclopedia of Alabama*, http://www.encyclopediaofalabama.org/article/h-2152.

Lincecum, Gideon. "Autobiography of Gideon Lincecum." *Publications of the Mississippi Historical Society* 8 (Oxford: Mississippi Historical Society, 1905), 443–519.

Lowery, Charles D. "The Great Migration to the Mississippi Territory, 1798–1819." *Journal of Mississippi History* 30 (August 1968): 173–92.

———. "The Great Migration to the Mississippi Territory, 1798–1819." *Mississippi History Now*, November 2000, http://mshistorynow.mdah.state.ms.us/articles/169/the-great-migration-to-the-mississippi-territory-1798-1819.

Lowry, Lucile Cary. "Lafayette's Visit to Georgia and Alabama." *Alabama Historical Quarterly* 8 (Spring 1946): 35–40.

Lyon, Anne Bozeman. "The Bonapartists in Alabama." *Alabama Historical Quarterly* 25 (Fall and Winter 1963): 227–41.

Martin, John M. "The Early Career of Gabriel Moore." *Alabama Historical Quarterly* 29 (Fall and Winter 1967): 89–105.

Matthias, Virginia Parks. "Natchez-Under-the-Hill: As It Developed under the Influence of the Mississippi River and the Natchez Trace." *Journal of Mississippi History* 7 (1945): 201–21.

McLemore, Richard A. "The Division of the Mississippi Territory." *Journal of Mississippi History* 5 (1943): 79–82.

McLemore, Richard, and Nannie McLemore. "The Birth of Mississippi." *Journal of Mississippi History* 39 (November 1967): 255–69.

McMillan, Malcom Cook. "The Alabama Constitution of 1819: A Study of Constitution-Making on the Frontier." *Alabama Review* 3 (October 1950): 263–85.

McMurtrie, Douglas C. "A Note on Joseph P. Forster, Pioneer Alabama Printer." *Alabama Historical Quarterly* 5 (Summer 1943): 234–36.

McWilliams, Tennant S. "The Marquis and the Myth: Lafayette's Visit to Alabama, 1825." *Alabama Review* 22 (April 1969): 135–45.

Mellown, Robert O. "Steamboats in Alabama." *Encyclopedia of Alabama*, http://www.encyclopediaofalabama.org/article/h-1803.

Moore, Margaret Deschamps. "Protestantism in the Mississippi Territory." *Journal of Mississippi History* 29 (November 1967): 358–70.

Morton, William J. "Exploring the Mystery of Famed Surveyor Thomas Freeman: Just Who Was the Man Who Worked Alongside Famous U.S. Surveyor Andrew Ellicott?" *Point of Beginning*, http://www.pobonline.com/articles/97502-exploring-the-mystery-of-thomas-freeman.

Nelms, Jack N. "Early Days with the Alabama River Steamboats." *Alabama Review* 37 (January 1984): 13–23.

Nuermberger, Ruth Ketring. "The 'Royal Party' in Early Alabama Politics." *Alabama Review* 6 (April 1953): 83–95 and (July 1953): 200–212.

O'Brien, Greg. "Chickasaws in Alabama." *Encyclopedia of Alabama*, http://www.encyclopediaofalabama.org/article/h-1487.

———. "Choctaws in Alabama." *Encyclopedia of Alabama*, http://www.encyclopediaofalabama.org/article/h-1186.

Otto, John Solomon. "The Migration of the Southern Plain Folk: An Interdisciplinary Synthesis." *Journal of Southern History* 51 (May 1985): 183–200.

Owen, Thomas McAdory. "The Genesis of the University of Alabama." *Alabama Historical Quarterly* 2 (Summer 1940): 169–88.

———, ed. "The Visit of President James Monroe to Alabama Territory, June 1, 1819." In *Transactions of the Alabama Historical Society, 1898–1899*, 154–58. Tuscaloosa: Alabama Historical Society, 1899.

Owsley, Frank L. "The Pattern of Migration and Settlement on the Southern Frontier." *Journal of Southern History* 11 (May 1945): 147–76.

Owsley, Frank L., Jr. "Benjamin Hawkins, the First Modern Indian Agent." *Alabama Historical Quarterly* 30 (Summer 1968): 7–14.

———. "British and Indian Activities in Spanish West Florida during the War of 1812." *Florida Historical Quarterly* 46 (October 1967): 111–23.

Parker, James C. "Blakeley: A Frontier Seaport." *Alabama Review* 27 (January 1974): 39–51.

———. "Fort Jackson after the War of 1812." *Alabama Review* 38 (April 1985): 119–30.

Pearson, Theodore Bowling. "Early Settlement around Historic McIntosh Bluff: Alabama's First County Seat." *Alabama Review* 23 (October 1970): 243–55.

Phelps, Dawson A. "Colbert Ferry and Selected Documents." *Alabama Historical Quarterly* 25 (Fall and Winter 1963): 203–26.

———. "The Natchez Trace in Alabama." *Alabama Review* 7 (January 1954): 28–37.

Phillips, Kenneth E., and Janet Roberts. "Cotton." *Encyclopedia of Alabama*, http://www.encyclopediaofalabama.org/article/h-1491.

Pruitt, Paul McWhorter, Jr. "Harry Toulmin." *Encyclopedia of Alabama*, http://www.encyclopediaofalabama.org/article/h-3108.

Riley, Franklin L. "Location of the Boundaries of Mississippi." *Publications of the Mississippi Historical Society* 3 (1900): 167–84.

Roberts, Frances C. "Dr. David Moore, Urban Pioneer of the Old Southwest." *Alabama Review* 18 (January 1965): 37–46.

———. "Politics and Public Land Disposal in Alabama's Formative Period." *Alabama Review* 22 (July 1969): 163–74.

———. "Thomas Freeman—Surveyor of the Old Southwest." *Alabama Review* 40 (July 1987): 216–31.

Rowland, Dunbar. "Military History of Mississippi, 1803–1898." In *The Official Statistical Register of the State of Mississippi, 1908*. Jackson: Mississippi Department of Archives and History, 1908.

Scott, John. "Cahaba: Hallowed Ground." *Alabama Heritage* (Winter 2011): 12–23.

Siebenthaler, Donna J. "Washington County." *Encyclopedia of Alabama*, http://www.encyclopediaofalabama.org/article/h-1295.

Smith, Susanna. "Washington, Mississippi: Antebellum Elysium." *Journal of Mississippi History* 40 (May 1978): 143–65.

Sprague, Stuart Seely. "Alabama Town Production during the Era of Good Feelings." *Alabama Historical Quarterly* 36 (Spring 1974): 15–20.

Stockham, Richard J. "The Misunderstood Lorenzo Dow." *Alabama Review* 16 (January 1963): 20–34.

Stumpf, Stuart O. "The Arrest of Aaron Burr: A Documentary Record." *Alabama Historical Quarterly* 42 (Fall and Winter 1980): 113–23.

Sugden, John. "Early Pan-Indianism: Tecumseh's Tour of the Indian Country, 1811–12." *American Indian Quarterly* (Fall 1986): 273–304.

Summersell, Charles Grayson. "Alabama and the Supreme Court: The First Case." *Alabama Review* 10 (July 1957): 163–75.

Thorn, Cecelia Jean. "The Bell Factory: Early Pride of Huntsville." *Alabama Review* 32 (January 1979): 28–37.

Thornton, J. Mills. "Broad River Group." *Encyclopedia of Alabama*, http://www.encyclopediaofalabama.org/article/h-1137.

"United States Land Offices in Alabama, 1803–1879." *Alabama Historical Quarterly* 17 (Fall 1955): 146–48.

Van Antwerp, Sidney. "Michael Portier, First Bishop of Mobile, 1795–1859." *Alabama Review* 24 (July 1971): 205–13.

Vejnar, Robert J. "Plantation Agriculture." *Encyclopedia of Alabama*, http://www.encyclopediaofalabama.org/article/h-1832.

Ward, Michael. "The Panic of 1819." *Encyclopedia of Alabama*, http://www.encyclopediaofalabama.org/article/h-2568.

Waselkov, Gregory. "Fort Mims Battle and Massacre." *Encyclopedia of Alabama*, http://www.encyclopediaofalabama.org/article/h-1121.

Watts, Charles W. "Colbert's Reserve and the Chickasaw Treaty of 1818." *Alabama Review* 7 (October 1959): 272–80.

West, Elizabeth Howard. "A Prelude to the Creek War of 1813–14." *Florida Historical Quarterly* 18 (April 1940): 247–66.

Wilkins, Jesse M. "Early Times in Wayne County." *Publications of the Mississippi Historical Society* 6 (1902): 265–72.

Williams, Clanton. "Conservatism in Old Montgomery, 1817–1861." *Alabama Review* 10 (April 1957): 96–110.

Williams, Jack K. "Crime and Punishment in Alabama, 1819–1840." *Alabama Review* 6 (January 1953): 14–30.

Wilson, Claire M. "Abraham Mordecai." *Encyclopedia of Alabama*, http://www.encyclopediaofalabama.org/article/h-3135.

Wunder, John. "American Law and Order Comes to the Mississippi Territory: The Making of Sargent's Code, 1798–1800." *Journal of Mississippi History* 38 (1976): 131–55.

INDEX

Page numbers in italics refer to illustrations.

A
Adams, David, 24
Adams, John, 6, 11
Adams, John Quincy, 81
agriculture, 49–51
Aigleville, 39
Alabama, 81
Alabama: climate and description, 31–32, 47–48; constitutional convention, 70–71; culture and society, 48–53; first legislature, 73–75; statehood, 75; towns in, 54–58
Alabama Central Female College, 119
Alabama Constitution Village, 100
"Alabama Fever." *See* immigration
Alabama Historical Commission, 105
Alabama River, 14, 22–23, 55, 65, 84–85, 111, 118, 132
Alabama Territory, 37, 38, 61, *62*, 67, 68, 76, 112, 114, 130; creation and borders, 61–62; move toward statehood, 70–71; politics and government in, 63–65
Allen, Ethan, 37
Alston-Cobb House, 131
Apalachicola River, 28
Ardmore, AL, 102
Asbury School and Mission, 83
Ashville, AL, 109
Assembly Hall, *13*, 97
Auburn, *94*, 95
Austill, Margaret Ervin, 35–36
Autauga County, AL, 77
Autossee, Battle of, 24

B
Beasley, Daniel, 21
Belle Mina, 100
Bell Tavern, 86, 120
Bibb, Thomas, 63–64; as governor, 77–78, 100
Bibb, William Wyatt, *63*, 63–65, 69, 73, 77, 85, 114; gravesite, 112, *113*
Bibb County, AL, 77
Big Spring Park, 101
Birmingham, AL, 108
Black Warrior River, 55, 85–86, 87
Blakeley, AL, 56, *57*, 82
Blakeley, Josiah, 56
Blakeley Sun, *44*, *81*
Blount County Historical Society, 107
Blow, Peter, 103
Bluff Hall, 116–17
Bradford, Henry C., 101
Breckinridge, Richard, 36–37
Broad River Group. *See* "Royal Party"
Burnt Corn Creek, Battle of, 21
Burr, Aaron, 14, *15*, 126
Burritt on the Mountain, 102

C
Cahaba River, 23, 55, 65, 77, 118
Cahawba (Cahaba), 2, 55, 65, 77–78, 82, 84–85, 118, 120
Cahawba County. *See* Bibb County

Cain, Joe, 126
Calabee Creek, Battle of, 25
Caller, James, 21
camp meetings. *See* religion
Canoe Fight, 22–23, *23*
Capitol Park, 119
Centreville, AL, 55–56
Chambers, Henry, 79
Chattahoochee Indian Heritage Center, 124
Chattahoochee River, 6, 8, 10, 15, 24, 83
Cherokee Indians, 10, 14, 26, 35, 66–68
Chickasaw Indians, 10, 14, 66–68
Choctaw Indians, 9–10, 14, 23, 66–68
Choctaw Trading House, 117
Chotard, Sarah F., 55
Church Street Graveyard, 126
Claiborne, AL, 84, 131–32
Claiborne, Ferdinand, 22–23, 118
Claiborne, W. C. C., 11–12
Clarke County, AL, 35, 130
Clarke County Historical Museum, 131
Cocke, John, 25
Coffee, John, 25–26, 55, 104
Colbert, George, 67, 97
Colbert, Levi, 67
Collier, Henry, 120
Collier-Overby House, 120
Condé-Charlotte House, 125, *126*
Conecuh County, AL, 115
Conecuh River, 132
Coosada, AL, 112
Coosa River, 15, 28
Cotaco County, AL, 65
cotton, 31, 42, 45–46, 50, 56, 60, 75
Coweta, 24
Crawford, William H., 64
Creek Indians, 10, 14–17, 66–69, 83–84
Creek War, 2, 19–28, 31, 35, 36, 48, 50, 55, 60, 77, 83, 98, 104, 108, 109, 114, 118, 124, 130, 132
Crocheron, David, 77
Crocheron, Nicholas, 77
Crockett, David, 26
Crowell, John, 64

D

Dale, Sam, 22, 83, 98, 124
Daphne, AL, 129
Decatur, AL, 105
DeFrance's Tavern. *See* Assembly Hall
Demopolis, AL, 39, 116–18
Douglas Hotel, 64
Dupre, Daniel S., 38

E

Eddins House, *102*
Edgewood, 112
Ellicott, Andrew, 6, 95, 127
Ellicott Stone, 127, *127*
Ely, William, 52, 85
Emuckfau Creek, Battle of, 26
Enitachopco Creek, Battle of, 26
Erskine House, 102
Escambia County, AL, 115

F

Federalist Party, 11–12
Federal Road, 16–17, 33, 84, 115
First Presbyterian Church of Tuscumbia, 104, *104*
First Seminole War, 69, 114, 132
Florence, AL, 32, 55, 103–4
Floyd, John, 24–25
Ford, John, 61, 98
Ford Home, 98
Forks of the Road Slave Market, 96, *96*
Fort Bibb, 69, 114
Fort Bowyer, 128
Fort Bowyer, Battle of, 28–30
Fort Carlota (Fort Charlotte), 8
Fort Claiborne, 23, 132
Fort Conde, 124
Fort Crawford, 69, 132
Fort Jackson, 28
Fort Mims, Battle of, 20–22, 25, 129, 130
Fort Mims State Historic Site, *129*, 129–30
Fort Mitchell, 24, 69, 83, 124
Fort Mitchell Historic Site, 124
Fort Payne, AL, 109
Fort Sinquefield, Battle of, 130–31
Fort Sinquefield Historical Park, 130
Fort Stoddert, 14, 126–27
Fort Toulouse – Fort Jackson Park, 114, *115*
Freeman, Thomas, 41
Friends of Historic Northport, 121

G
Gaines, Edmund P., 14, 126
Gaines, George S., 39–40, 68, 117
Gaineswood, 117
General John Coffee Cemetery, 104
Georgia, 6, 7, 16, 22, 24–25, 33, 34, 60, 61, 63, 68, 76, 79, 115
Globe Hotel, 130
Gloucester, 95
Governor Holmes House, 93
"Great Migration." *See* immigration
Greensboro, AL, 121–22
Greenwood, 122
Greenwood Cemetery, 121

H
Hall, Bolling, 83
Harding, Lyman, 95
Harriet, 82
Hawkins, Benjamin, 16, 19, 28
Hermes, 29
Hickman, John P., 105
Hickman log cabin, 105
Hickory Ground, 28
Hillsboro, AL, 105
Historic Blakeley State Park, 128, *128*
Historic Hale County Preservation Society, 122
Historic Jefferson College, 96, *97*
History Museum of Mobile, 124
Hitchcock, Henry, *36*, 36–38, 52
Hodges, AL, 105
Holmes, David, 45, 93
Holmes House, 93
Holy Ground, Battle of, 23, 118
Holy Ground Battlefield Park, 118
Horseshoe Bend, Battle of, 26–28
Horseshoe Bend National Military Park, 122–24, *123*
House on Ellicott Hill, *94*, 95
Huffman, AL, 108
Hunt, John, 34–35, 76, 101
Huntsville, AL, 10, 28, 34–35, 41, 53, 55, 61, 64, 65, 70, 73, 75, 76–77, 98, 100–102

I
immigration, 2, 31–44, 56, 115
Indian Springs Baptist Church, 132

J
Jackson, Andrew, *25*, 25–29, 56, 70, 80–81, 108, 122, 129
Jackson's Oak, 129
Jefferson, Thomas, 11–13
Jefferson County, AL, 37
Jude-Crutcher House, 102

K
Kimbell-James Massacre, 131
King, Edmund, 106
King, William Rufus de Vane, 70, 75, 119
King House, 106–7, *107*
Kirby, Ephraim, 51, 127

L
Lafayette, Marquis de, 82–84, *83*
Land Relief Act of 1821, 76
Lattimore, William, 60
Lauderdale County, AL, 65
Lawrence, William, 30
Lawrence County, AL, 65
Levasseur, Auguste, 82, 84
Limestone County, AL, 65
Lincecum, Gideon, 38
Linden, 95
log cabin: at Bluff Hall, 116, *117*; in Old Alabama Town, 110
Long, William, 77
Looney House, *49*, 109
Louisiana Purchase, 7–8, 12
Louisiana Territory. *See* Louisiana Purchase
Loveless, John, 107
Lucas Tavern, 109, *111*

M
Madison County, AL, 10, 39, 64–65, 70
Marengo County, AL, 39
Marion County Historical Society, 98
Marks, William Matthews, 114
Marks House, 114
Marmaduke Williams House, 120
Masonic Lodge #3, 131, *132*
McGuire, Moses, 120
McGuire-Strickland House, 120
McIntosh, Chilly, 68, 83
McIntosh, William, 83
Mead, Cowles, 13

Midway, AL, 115
Milledgeville, GA, 41
Mims, Samuel, 21
Mississippi, 82
Mississippi Department of Archives and History, 97
Mississippi River, 6, 8–10, 59, *92*, 93, 95
Mississippi Territory, 1–2, *7*, *9*, 19, 22, 25, 31, 35, 42, 45, 49, 91, 93, 95, 96, 98, 127, 130, 132; division of, 13, 59–61; formation and early growth, 6–11, 31–33; politics and government in, 11–13; sectional rivalry in, 13–14, 61
Mobile, AL, 5, 6, 8, 10, 14, 16, 28–30, 34, 37, 40, 42, 45, 52, 54, 56, *57*, 58, 59, 61, 82, 84, 115, 124–26, 128, 129
Mobile Bay, 1, 28, 48, 56, 82, 128
Mobile Medical Museum, 126
Mobile Point, 28, 84
Mobile River, 14, 127
Mobile-Tensaw Delta, 56
Monmouth, 95
Monroe, James, 63, 70, *74*, 75, 82
Monroe County, AL, 41, 69, 115, 132
Monte Sano Mountain, 102
Montgomery, AL, 11, 55, 82, 84, 87, 109, 110–12, 115, 119
Mooresville, AL, 98
Mordecai, Abraham, 11, 110
Morgan County, AL. *See* Cotaco County, AL
Mound Line Historic Marker, 130
Mount Locust Inn and Plantation, 97
Mount Vernon Arsenal and Barracks, 127
Mount Vernon Cantonment, 127
Murphree, Daniel, 107
Murphree log cabin, 107, *108*
Murphy, John, 80
Muscle Shoals, AL, 103–4
Museum of Alabama, 111, *112*

N

Napoleon Bonaparte, 39–40
Nashville, TN, 28
Natchez, MS, 6, 9–10, 11–12, 14, 22, 37, 42, 60; historic sites in, 91, 92–97
Natchez District, 9–10
Natchez Trace Visitor's Center, 97
Natchez-Under-the-Hill, 10
Natchez Visitor Center, 93
New Orleans, Battle of, 29
New Orleans, LA, 10, 12, 17, 29, 40, 42, 45, 82, 84
newspapers, 31, 56–57
New York, NY, 32
Nichols, William, 86
Noel-Ramsey House, 122

O

Oak Hill Cemetery, 108
Oakwood Cemetery, 111
Old Alabama Town, 109–11
Old Brick Presbyterian Church, 104
Old Cahawba Archaeological Park, 118
Old Saint Stephens Historical Park, 130, *131*
Old Tavern, 120, *121*
Oneonta, AL, 107
Opothle Yoholo, *69*
Orleans Territory, 12
Overton, Abner, 105
Overton Farm, 105, *105*

P

Palisades Park, 107
Panic of 1819, 75–76, 79
Pascagoula, MS, 61
Pearl River, 8, 10, 13, 61
Pearl River Convention, 61, 98
Pensacola, FL, 6, 19, 21, 29, 129
Perdido River, 8
Perteat, Solomon, 121
Phelps-Jones House, 102
Phenix City, AL, 115
Pickens, Israel, 78–80, *79*, 84, 122
Pickett, Albert James, 88
Pike Road, AL, 114
Pinckney, Thomas, 28
Planters and Merchants Bank, 64, 76, 80
Poindexter, George, 60
Pond Spring, 105
Pope, LeRoy, 64, 76, 101
Pope Mansion, 101
Pope's Tavern and Museum, 103, *103*
Port Gibson, MS, 9
Public Inn, 101

Q
Quitman, John A., 95

R
Red Sticks. *See* Creek Indians
Reed, William, 108
Reed-Riddle-Jemison House, 108
religion, 52–54
Republican Party, 11
Revolutionary War, 6, 9, 37
Richmond, VA, 14
Rock Creek Canyon Equestrian Park, 105
Royall, Anne, 48, 67
"Royal Party," 64, 76, 79
Russell, Gilbert C., 23

S
Sadler Plantation House, 107
Saint Clair County Historical Society, 109
Saint Domingue (Haiti), 39
Saint James CME Church, 118, *119*
Saint Stephens, AL, 38, 41, 64, 78, 82, 130
Saint Stephens Academy, 64
Saint Stephens Steamboat Company, 82
Sam Dale Memorial, 124
Sam Dale Monument, 98
Sargent, Winthrop, 11–12, *12*, 95
"Sargent's Code," 11
Scott, Dred, 103
Second Bank of the United States, 75
Second Creek War, 87
Selma, AL, 55, 75, 84, 119
Sequoyah, 67–68, 109
slavery, 41–46
Smith, Isaac, 83
Stagecoach Inn and Tavern, 98, *99*
steamboats, 81–82

T
Tait, Charles, 61, 64, 70
Talladega, AL, 108
Tallapoosa River, 15, 24–25, 26, 28, 114, 122
Tallassee, AL, 114
Tallushatchee, Battle of, 25–26
Tecumseh, *16*, 16–17, 114
Tennessee, 6, 8, 19, 22, 25, 26, 28, 34, 35, 36, 61, 97, 109
Tennessee River, 10, *32*, 35, 61, 67, 85, 101
Tensa, 82
Tensaw River, 10, 19, 51, 56, 128
Tenskwatawa, 17
Texada, 93
Titus, James, 64
Tohopeka. *See* Horseshoe Bend, Battle of
Tombeckbe Bank, 64, 78
Tombigbee River, 10, 19, 22, 37, 38, 39, 61, 81
Toulmin, Harry, 14, 41, 98
Travis, William B., 131–32
Travis House, 131–32
Treaty of Fort Adams, 9
Treaty of Fort Jackson, 28, *60*
Treaty of Ghent, 30
Treaty of San Lorenzo, 6, 95
Tuckaubatchee, 17, 114
Tuscaloosa, AL, 2, 38, 55, 65, 80, 85–88, 119–21
Tuscumbia, AL, 103–5

U
Umbria Schoolhouse, 121, *122*
University of Alabama, 80
University of Montevallo, 106
US Army Corps of Engineers, 118

V
Vicksburg, MS, 9
Village, The. *See* Daphne, AL
Village Point Park Preserve, 128–29
Vincent, Benjamin, 126
Vincent-Walsh House, 126
Vine and Olive Colony, 39–40, 117–18, 122
Vischer, Lukas, 68

W
Walker, James, 120
Walker, John W., 64, 70, 75
Walnut Hills. *See* Vicksburg
War of 1812, 7, 8, 28–31, 127, 128, 129
Washington, George, 41, 82
Washington, Georges, 82
Washington, MS, 12–13
Washington County, AL, 10, 14, 61, 130
Weatherford, Sehoy Tate, 130
Weatherford, William, 21, 23, 28, 118; gravesite, 130

Weeden, Maria Howard, 101
Weeden, William, 101
Weeden House, *100*, 101
West, Cato, 13
West Florida, colony of, 6–8, 14, 127, 130
West Florida Rebellion, 8
West Jefferson County Historical Society, 107
Wheeler, General Joe, 105
White, James, 77
Whitfield, Nathan Bryan, 117
Wilkinson, James, 8, 29
Williams, Marmaduke, 120
Williams, Robert, 13
Wills Town Mission, 109
Woodville, MS, 10

Y
Yazoo Fraud, 6–7
Yazoo River, 6